FROM EARLY JUDAISM
TO EARLY CHURCH

FROM EARLY JUDAISM
TO EARLY CHURCH

D. S. RUSSELL

Fortress Press   Philadelphia

Library of Congress Cataloging-in-Publication Data

Russell, D. S. (David Syme), 1916–
  From early Judaism to early Church.

  Includes indexes.
  1. Judaism—History—Post-exilic period, 586 B.C.–
210 A. D.   2. Christianity—Early church, ca. 30–600.
I. Title.
BM176.R825   1986   220   85–31776
ISBN 0–8006–1921–8

2526A86   Printed in the United Kingdom   1–1921

Contents

Preface

It is now more than twenty-five years since I nervously produced my first little book *Between the Testaments* (SCM Press and Fortress Press 1960). Somewhat more ambitious volumes followed in which an attempt was made to expound the content and meaning of Jewish apocalyptic and to understand what, if any, is its abiding message, not least in terms of the Christian Gospel. Other writers have done this at much greater length and with much greater thoroughness and have demonstrated a renewed interest in apocalyptic during these intervening years, not least in the fields of New Testament study and systematic theology.

This present volume is as modest as the first in size and aim, though more comprehensive in its subject-matter. It examines a selection of topics which might have been dealt with in that first volume but were not. In some ways it overlaps the other, but its intention is to complement and supplement what was written there and in so doing to focus attention on just a few subjects which continue to be matters of interest and debate among scholars and students alike. The inclusion of these particular subjects is selective. As the title implies, it is an attempt to sketch certain aspects of the Judaism of those early years out of which the early church arose and by so doing to indicate Christianity's indebtedness to it and at the same time its own distinctive message.

It has not been written with the expert or the specialist in mind, but rather the student, the minister and lay person who wishes to understand a bit more clearly some of the religious developments that took place within the Judaism of roughly 200 BC – AD 100, and what influence these may have had on the mind of Jesus and his followers, on the writing of the Gospels and Epistles and on the ongoing mission of the early church. It is hoped that the reader, as a result of his or her perusal of this book, will be encouraged to delve more deeply into the subjects here discussed.

I am indebted to the Revd Harry Mowvley for reading the manuscript through and making most helpful comments, to Mrs Pat Miles for her ready assistance in deciphering my handwriting and preparing a clean copy for publication, and to my wife for her patience and constant encouragement.

Bristol, 1985   D. S. RUSSELL

I

Cultural and Religious Developments in the Hellenistic Age

I. A CHANGING CULTURAL PATTERN

(a) One culture, one world

The period between the rise of Alexander the Great (356–323 BC) and the birth of Christ was one of the most remarkable periods in ancient history, to be compared in not a few respects with the age in which we ourselves are now living. Alexander set himself the task of bringing into one the civilizations of East and West on the basis of that Greek culture, commonly designated by the word 'Hellenism', which he himself had inherited and of which he was an avowed champion. National, political and cultural barriers were thrown down in his triumphant march eastwards towards India; men of diverse customs and traditions were made to feel that they belonged together within 'the inhabited world' (*oikumene*). The ecumenical movement in his day included within its scope not just 'religion' but the whole of life. The prospect of world government, which many would regard as an ideal for humanity, was in great measure actually realized by Alexander and his immediate successors, the Ptolemies and the Seleucids.

Greek culture had, of course, been widely experienced and expressed long before his time. Writing on the rise and diffusion of Hellenic culture in the world of the fifth century BC to the time of Christ, W. F. Albright reminds us that 'after 500 BC came a burst of cultural progress unexampled in history which in half a century brought Attica to the age of Pericles, to the drama of Aeschylus,

1

Sophocles and Euripides, the sculpture of Phidias and the painting of Polygnotus. . . . It was about to reach heights of philosophical and scientific thought which were to usher in a new era in human history' (*From the Stone Age to Christianity*, 1957, p.335). Alexander accelerated the process already begun, setting himself to teach Greeks and Asiatics to accept each other as partners in a common culture by establishing Greek cities and colonies all over his great empire with their gymnasiums, stadiums, hippodromes and theatres as well as their method of government by democratic senate and by encouraging mixed marriages. The rapid spread of *koine* ('common') Greek greatly facilitated this process of Hellenization, for within a relatively short space of time it became the *lingua franca* of his great empire. Jews, of course, had met Greeks long before the time of Alexander; but it was from this time onwards that the Greek culture, in its Hellenistic form, began to have such an influence on all things Jewish.

(b) An age of syncretism

It was an age of cultural and religious syncretism in which all the inhabitants of the civilized world – Jews included – were inevitably involved. The account given by the Jewish historian Josephus concerning a Jewish sage of the middle of the fourth century BC is enlightening in this respect. His description of the meeting of this Jew with Aristotle is no doubt fictitious, but the substance of the story provides an interesting insight. This is how he narrates it:

> Not only did the Greeks know the Jews, but they admired any of their number whom they happened to meet. This statement applies not to the lowest class of Greeks, but to those with the highest reputation for wisdom, and can easily be proved. Clearchus, a disciple of Aristotle, and in the very first rank of peripatetic philosophers, relates, in his first book on Sleep, the following anecdote told of a certain Jew by his master. He puts the words into the mouth of Aristotle himself; . . . the man was a Jew of Coele-Syria. These people are descended from the Indian philosophers. The philosophers, they say, are in India called Calani, in Syria by the territorial name of Jews; for the

district which they inhabit is known as Judaea. Their city has a remarkably odd name: they call it Hierusaleme. Now this man, who was entertained by a large circle of friends and was on his way down from the interior to the coast, not only spoke Greek, but had the soul of a Greek. During my stay in Asia, he visited the same places as I did, and came to converse with me and some other scholars, to test our learning. But as one who had been intimate with many cultivated persons, it was rather he who imparted to us something of his own (*Against Apion* I, 176–181).

Further information is given about this historically obscure period in the so-called Zeno papyri which include the correspondence of one Zeno, an agent of Apollonius, chief finance minister to Ptolemy II (285–247 BC), supplemented by the so-called Vienna papyri relating to approximately the same period. Together they help to fill an otherwise blank space in Jewish history and give a good picture of the close contact at that time between Palestine and Egypt and of the administrative control of Palestine by officials representing the authorities in Alexandria. These papyri provide a good barometer indicating the pressure of Hellenization to which Jews, both in Palestine and in Egypt, were subjected during these years. This is seen, for example, in the marriage of soldiers and other settlers in Syria and Phoenicia with native women and the consequent fusion of Western and Eastern populations. Of particular significance in this connection is the evidence of certain legal papyri relating to the situation in Egypt showing that, although the Jews were permitted to live according to their own ancestral laws, they made full use of Hellenistic law as, for example, in the matter of marriage and divorce. Of special interest is the reference in these papyri to a Jew called Tobias (Hebrew, *Tobiah*) who is described as a man of great wealth and commander of a military colony of Ptolemaic soldiers in Transjordan. In a letter addressed to Apollonius he gives the customary Greek formula of greeting, 'Many thanks to the gods', the use of the plural indicating the degree to which his Jewish faith in the one God had been compromised. Noting the influence Tobias's descendants were yet to have on Jewish affairs Victor Tcherickover makes this remark:

'Hellenization begins with the "contamination" of the Tobiad family by things of no importance such as pagan formulae in correspondence, probably with the changing of names (from Hebrew to Greek), the learning of Greek and the like, and leads in the third generation (the sons of Joseph, Tobias's son) to a spurning of tradition and an attempt to introduce a thorough-going Hellenistic reform' (*Hellenistic Civilisation and the Jews*, 1961, p.71).

The subsequent story of Joseph the Tobiad and his son Hyrcanus bears all this out. To maintain a position of influence and wealth in the community required compliance with Greek ways, and this they were willing to do. Social standing took precedence over religious scruple. Rivalries between the house of the Tobiads and the high priestly house of the Oniads led eventually to a widening of the gap between the 'Hellenizers' and those who stood by 'the laws of their fathers'.

(c) A composite culture

Beneath the surface of this syncretistic Hellenism the old Eastern religions of Babylonia and Persia, for example, continued to exercise a powerful influence. This is not surprising, for when Alexander took over the Persian Empire (which itself had taken over the Babylonian Empire) and pressed on towards India he made a breach in the barrier separating East and West through which (in the words of S. B. Frost) there 'came flooding back the lore and "wisdom" of the east . . . a Greek-philosophized blend of Iranian esotericism and Chaldean astrology and determinism' (*Old Testament Apocalyptic*, 1952, pp. 75f.). Prominent ingredients in this highly syncretistic culture were such things as occultism, magic, astrology, demonology, angelology, cosmology, anthropology, and eschatology. These left their mark on the life and thought of the Jewish people as a whole, particularly in the Dispersion, but to a large extent also in Palestine which, apart from a limited area around Jerusalem, could for much of this time be said to belong to the Dispersion also, where the impact of Hellenism upon it at least was concerned. In any case, during this long period it is more than likely that many Jews who had lived all their lives in Mesopotamia in direct contact with Perso-Babylonian thought and culture were attracted back to

4

Palestine, e.g. during and after the period of the Maccabees, as they witnessed the establishment of a strong Jewish state.

The extent to which Persian and Hellenistic influence is to be found in the writings of the intertestamental period, particularly those of an apocalyptic kind (see ch. 7), is a continuing point of debate among scholars. As evidence of such influence reference has been made to the interest shown in many such writings in astrology and cosmology; the frequently expressed belief in angels and demons; and the development of a form of eschatology different from that to be found in the Old Testament itself. It has been cogently argued, however, that influence of this kind was relatively late and that the basic beliefs and imagery of apocalyptic are in fact native to Hebrew tradition and continue the line of Hebrew prophecy.

Alongside this Syrian type of Hellenism went that of Egypt under the Ptolemies. Here the old mystical traditions of Egypt and Babylon were confronted by the new Greek sciences, producing a form of culture and belief much more abstract than that of its Syrian counterpart, and a philosophical expression of religion which is amply illustrated in a number of Jewish writings of this period. Such influence showed itself, as in the case of the Jews of Palestine and the rest of the Dispersion, not only among those who were themselves sympathetic towards the Hellenistic culture, but even among those who were, to all appearances, radically opposed to it. A hint of this is given by Josephus who, in passing as it were, indicates that the Essenes (a strict Jewish community) lived the same kind of life as those whom the Greeks called Pythagoreans (*Antiquities* XV.x.4). He probably had in mind in particular the Pythagorean conception of the orderliness of the universe as embodied in the observance of a solar calendar and their practice of purifications, both of which played an important part in the system of life and belief adopted at Qumran.

(d) Reaction against Hellenism

Under the Ptolemies and Seleucids, Alexander's successors, a policy of toleration was pursued allowing Judaism and Hellenism to co-exist. It was a time of considerable danger to those who were jealous to maintain the tradition of their fathers. Many willingly embraced the Greek culture, with its often compromising rites and ceremonies, the predecessors of the Sadducees in particular showing great readiness to accommodate themselves to the ways of their rulers. Others were unconsciously pressurized into line; it was in the very air they breathed, in the buildings and statues around them, in local politics, in the sports they played, in the books they read, in their social life and in their religious life as well. Even the most exclusive among them could not but be influenced deeply, for good or for ill.

Matters came to a head in the time of the Seleucid ruler, Antiochus IV (175–163 BC) who, fearful of the break-up of his kingdom, instigated a vigorous policy of Hellenization in an attempt to weld it more securely together. Socially and culturally the Jews must have been deeply affected, living for the most part as they did in the Dispersion, in a heathen 'secular' environment. Under pressure from Antiochus and with the support of the Hellenizing Jewish party in Jerusalem a gymnasium – a popular symbol and expression of Hellenism – was built in the city itself. Jewish youths (young priests among them) enrolled and took part in the games. Many wore the distinctive cap of Hermes, the patron of Greek sports, and athletes tried to remove the mark of circumcision so as to avoid the derision of the crowds. According to II Maccabees 4.11 the right of the Jews to live according to their ancestral laws was abrogated and Jerusalem was given over to the Greek way of life. All this had serious religious implications for the Jews. Some of the influences were insidious; others were quite open as in the case of the games in the gymnasiums which were normally accompanied by sacrifices to heathen gods.

When Antiochus interfered in the appointment of a high priest of his own choosing, fighting broke out in the city. The king bitterly resented this challenge to his own authority and determined to teach the Jews a lesson. He desecrated the temple and plundered its treasures. The Syrian soldiers, devotees of the god Baal Shamen ('Lord of Heaven') appropriated the temple precincts for their own syncretistic worship so that the worship of heathen gods went on alongside that of the God of Israel. In all this they actually found support among the Hellenizing Jews. But Antiochus had not yet completed his evil designs: he decided to exterminate the Jewish religion altogether. In 167 BC he issued a proclamation forbidding the people to live any longer according to their ancestral laws. The distinctive marks of the Jewish faith were proscribed on penalty of death – the observance of the traditional sacrifices and festivals, the rite of circumcision and the reading of the Law. To crown this infamy, in December 167 BC, he set up in the temple an altar to the Olympian Zeus on top of the altar of burnt offerings and ordered that swine's flesh be offered on it (cf. II Maccabees 6.2; Daniel 11.31; 12.11).

The story of the Maccabean revolt and the re-dedication of the temple in 164 BC is a familiar one. The Hellenizers seemed to have been thwarted. But in truth we see in the Hasmonaean house, which held secular and religious power from the time of Judas Maccabaeus onwards for many years, the corroding influence of 'secularization', influenced deeply by the Hellenistic climate which continued to prevail. And when, in course of time and with the help of the Romans, the power passed into the hands of Herod (37–4 BC) and his sons, the policy of Hellenization went on at an even greater pace. He replaced the old hereditary aristocracy with one of his own and adopted a centralized bureaucracy along Hellenistic lines. He built a theatre in Jerusalem and a great amphitheatre in the plain beyond. He encouraged the cult of the emperor and had statues erected to himself throughout his kingdom.

Some years after the close of his reign (in AD 6) the party of the Zealots was born who symbolized the burning hatred felt by many Jews both for Herod and his family and also for the Roman procurators (AD 6–66) who governed the land. To them, and to many others, the struggle was a holy war which reached its terrible climax in the so-called Jewish War of AD 66–70, when Jerusalem was destroyed and the Jewish state ceased to exist. The only attempt made subsequently in AD 132 under one Ben Kosebah (Bar Kochba) proved to be abortive and Jerusalem was re-founded as a Gentile city with the new name of Aelia Capitolina. Entry was banned to every Jew on penalty of death.

Throughout these long years the struggle to preserve Judaism continued unabated. Some felt they had to resist all encroachments of Hellenism as 'pollutions' and 'abominations' and to uphold at all costs 'the laws of their fathers'. Others were deeply influenced by much that they saw and heard, consciously or unconsciously, and found their faith enriched thereby. Others again fell away from their religion or renounced their faith. Hellenism was a powerful force with a tremendous appeal, not least to the priestly aristocracy in Jerusalem. But Judaism remained, changed no doubt and tempered as by fire. Many remained true to 'the covenant' and to 'the law of their fathers' and so prepared the way for Judaism's own survival and, alongside that, the birth of the Christian church.

2. RELIGIOUS DEVELOPMENTS

(a) Temple and Torah

The greatest support for Hellenism among the Jews came from the wealthier sections of the community among whom the priestly aristocracy were numbered. Such people stood to gain most from its success, for Hellenism carried with it economic and social as well as cultural and religious implications. The priestly class, led by the high priest, were in control of the temple, which was the focal point of life and worship for the whole Jewish people. Jerusalem itself assumed the character of a temple-state. In both temple and Gerousia (later to develop under the name 'Sanhedrin'), the high priest occupied a position of supreme importance. It is not surprising to discover that, sharing as they did in both the wealth and the authority of this temple-state, the priestly aristocracy were peculiarly vulnerable to the influence of Hellenism and soon gained the reputation of being among its staunchest supporters.

Now, as custodians of the temple worship they were at the same time guardians and exponents of the Pentateuch which had been handed down through Ezra the priest and speedily gained an authoritative standing within Judaism. This Law Book was of particular relevance to their own function on two grounds: it had much to say about the proper ordering of temple worship and about the responsibility of a hereditary priesthood to interpret and apply

8

its regulations. The priestly class, under the high priest, accepted this responsibility in their generation and sought to work it out along two lines: they took great pains to ensure that the priestly rules laid down in the Law Book concerning ritual 'purity' were carried out to the letter, and they emphasized the complete separation of God's holy people Israel from all the 'unclean' Gentile nations round about. By these two means, ritual purity and separation, the people would show their obedience to the Law and thereby their faithfulness to the covenant which God had made with Moses at Sinai long ago. As interpreters and practitioners of such teaching the priestly class claimed for itself a unique place of authority both religiously and politically.

But such a claim was not to go unchallenged. The challenge, when it came, followed two lines. The first concerned their right alone to interpret the Law: they had compromised their position as teachers of the Law by allowing themselves to become corrupted by influences from outside which seemed to contradict the very things for which they said they stood and had forfeited their right to claim a monopoly as interpreters of the mind of God as revealed in the Torah. A new system of interpretation was called for which would apply the laws of God to the life of the people in a new way, a new system in which laymen as well as priests would be able to participate. And so we find the development of 'schools' of 'the wise' with their teaching concerning the correspondence or otherwise between divine justice and the governance of the universe, the growth of synagogues with their emphasis on the study of Torah and its application to the lives of ordinary men and the growth of the apocalyptic tradition with its interpretation of scripture in the light of secret revelation.

The second challenge concerned their control of religious rites and ceremonies by virtue of their exclusive claim to control the temple cultus. The results of this can be seen in the years following the Maccabaean revolt in the emergence in Judaism of a number of groupings or parties, the emphasis of whose teaching lay in the Torah rather than the temple, with institutions and ceremonies of their own, or who withdrew from the temple altogether and formed select religious communities as at Qumran near the shores of the Dead Sea.

(b) Parties in Judaism

The influential group of wealthy and powerful men, to whom reference has been made, formed a social aristocracy, then, within which were numbered the high priest and other leading priestly officials of the old Zadokite line. In later years they were to emerge as the party of the Sadducees, a name which has been variously taken to signify 'Zadok-ones' or 'righteous-ones' or 'Syndics', a Greek term signifying people who defend the existing laws against innovation. The actual name appears on record for the first time in the days of John Hyrcanus (134–104 BC) in connection with the breach between him and the Pharisees, but it is clear that both parties originated at a much earlier time than this and were established as recognizable rival parties not long after the Maccabaean revolt (168 BC). The Sadducees were conservative in both politics and religion, doing their best to maintain the existing social and political order and, as we have seen, championing the observance of the temple ritual and the right of the priests to interpret the Law. They maintained that the Torah alone was authoritative, without denying the sacredness of the other scriptures, and so rejected certain doctrines such as that of bodily resurrection which found no justification in the Law.

There is reason to think that the Pharisees (together with the Essenes) may trace back their common spiritual origin to the Hasidim or Pious Ones who gave their support to Judas Maccabaeus for a short time until religious freedom was won. In terms of lineal descent they are probably to be seen as successors of a class of scribes, chiefly lay, who set themselves the task of interpreting and applying the Law in the radically changed circumstances of their day. The priestly scribes found it impossible to cope with the flood of new customs and ideas prevailing during the Greek period and found their responsibilities as interpreters of the Law being challenged as never before.

Be that as it may, the Pharisees (essentially a lay movement, but with some priests among them) gained dominance in the schools and synagogues where they set themselves to interpret the Torah in such a way that it spoke not just to the formal worship of the temple and the ordering of festivals and sacrifices, but to the life of the people in its every aspect. The guidance they gave was both flexible and practical and stood in marked contrast to the rigid and ritual priestly pronouncements. Their emphasis, however, on ritual purity was no less strong and was applied right across the board to almost every aspect of life. Bit by bit there grew up an oral tradition containing the judgments and pronouncements of Rabbis and other religious leaders in succeeding generations covering almost every eventuality which later was to find written form in the Mishnah. This tradition the Pharisees regarded as of equal authority with the Torah itself.

Their study of the prophets led them to believe in the coming of a messianic kingdom in which the ancient House of David would be restored and in which also the righteous dead would share in resurrection. In the expression of such a belief they were not particularly militant, but it is of interest to observe that, according to the Jewish historian Josephus, one of the founder members of the militant Zealot party, which, as we have seen, came into existence in AD 6 was himself a Pharisee. These Zealots were prepared to resist with force foreign intrusion in the life and institutions of their nation and violently opposed the collaboration shown by the Herodians and the priestly rulers with the alien Roman authorities of that time.

The Essenes to whom, there is reason to believe, the Qumran community belonged, gave much time to the study of the Torah and to an interpretation of it different from that of either the Sadducees or Pharisees. They claimed to be persecuted by the ruling priestly families, and so deserted Jerusalem and lived among the villages or in remote deserts and caves, so that by the first century BC they had virtually become a monastic order. They adopted an ascetic life and devoted themselves to the ritual fulfilment of the Torah.

The Dead Sea Scrolls indicate that at Qumran the community was governed by a priestly hierarchy; their festivals were governed by a solar calendar; they laid great store by ritual worship and sacred

11

meals; and ritual purity was their constant concern. According to Josephus they sent gifts to the temple in Jersalem and offered sacrifices, but only under very special conditions of purity lest they incur ritual contamination. They, too, believed in the coming of a messianic kingdom with features familiar to us from some at least of the apocalyptic writing of the period.

These are only some (albeit the most important) of the many groupings within Judaism during these years which helped to shape the religious life and beliefs of the Jewish people in the years preceding the Christian era. One only was to remain when the others disappeared. The Pharisees had a chequered history throughout these long years, but in the rabbinic tradition they survived even the collapse of Jerusalem itself.

(c) Purification and separation

It will have become plain that two closely related matters, among others, were given high priority by the major parties within Judaism at this time. One was the need to safeguard against ritual impurity and the other to maintain a position of separation from people and things that were regarded as a pollution and unclean. The Pharisees in particular, as we have seen, sought to preserve ritual purity not only in matters relating to temple worship, but also to everyday relationships – in the home, in business and in the communities in which they met. In respect of the temple, following the example of Ezra, they took great care to maintain the pure priestly lineage and insisted that the head of state be of pure Jewish stock. On both counts they found themselves clashing with the authorities on a number of decisions throughout the Hasmonaean and Herodian eras. But their influence was more marked outside the temple and its ordering. In a whole multitude of situations they sought to define what was pure and what was impure and by so doing to put a fence, as it were, round dangerous areas. In this way they taught the need for separation not just from the Gentiles but also from situations, objects and people which might be a cause of contamination.

Their teaching in this regard was based on the Pentateuch and, within that, on the so-called Law of Holiness (Lev. 17–26) which describes Israel as a holy (or 'separated') nation and relates to such matters as the eating of clean as against unclean animals, the proper observance of festivals, entry into lawful marriages and what constitutes purification and pollution. In the Pentateuch itself eleven principal categories of pollution are listed which the Pharisees applied and elaborated as tests over a wide range of situations – personal, domestic and national. Just a few illustrations of their way of working may be given here.

Contact with a dead body resulted in a state of ritual impurity. Not content with such a broad statement, the Pharisees set about defining with precision exactly in what circumstances defilement would be brought about. Thus it is said that such defilement would be incurred if the contact was even with a bone of the dead body as large as a barley-corn or with a portion of flesh the size of an olive!

In the preparation of foods their own members had to exercise great care in their use of vessels which might have become ritually unclean and in their observance of the law of tithes which was closely associated with the maintenance of the priesthood. With this in mind they must be careful to purchase their foodstuffs only from 'reputable' traders and farmers who were not themselves in a state of impurity and to ensure that no one prepared their meals who might be in a state of defilement. This was a reference to the 'boorish' people of the land, many of whom lived in a perpetual state of ritual defilement if judged by the standards of the Pharisaic law.

In the case of pollutions, recourse was taken to purificatory rites of several kinds in which sprinkling with water or immersion in water played an important part. This applied to utensils as well as people. No one, for example, was allowed to enter the temple court until he had bathed, just in case he might have incurred pollution; and proselytes, being regarded as unclean, had likewise to submit to this purifying process.

The Law laid down, moreover, that no work should be carried out on the Sabbath day. The Pharisees sought to elucidate this and so in the early days of the Hasmonaean period we find a code indicating twenty-two types of work which are forbidden, later to be expanded to thirty-nine. Sometimes, however, the requirement is relaxed, as when the Seleucids attacked the Jews on the Sabbath and slew two thousand of them, or in the case of a person so ill that if help were not given he might very well die. Less meritorious were the rules permitting the transfer of food from one place to another. The sabbath laws allowed such transfer within households or estates; the Pharisees overcame this restriction by extending the 'estate' a distance of two thousand cubits or by including in it the courtyard between houses. (For other illustrations see Asher Finkel, *The Pharisees and the Teacher of Nazareth*, 1964 pp. 42ff.)

It was perhaps inevitable that such emphasis should lead to a measure of legalism and exclusivism not only in respect of the nations and peoples round about but even in respect of their own fellow-religionists. Nevertheless the Pharisees did much to 'democratize' religion, to make it the concern of the people whom they sought to teach the Law of God, and in so doing established for themselves a reputation for true piety and devotion.

(d) Religious ideas

It must be borne in mind that the 'parties' in Judaism which have been mentioned, influential though they were, represented only a relatively small percentage of the Jewish people at that time and that no one of them could claim to represent the 'norm' for 'orthodox' Judaism as became possible in the years following the fall of Jerusalem in AD 70. The fact is that during the intertestamental period there were many groups and splinter-groups, studying the Torah, practising the rites and ceremonies of their religion with meticulous care, pondering the meaning of life and the providence of God, and, in the case of some, putting into writing their hopes and fears. The literature thus produced is of importance for the light it throws on the development of certain religious ideas within Judaism and subsequently for the influence of these ideas in the early Christian church.

One such idea concerns the presence of evil in the world and the vindication of a good and righteous God in face of so much injustice and suffering. The quest for the origin of evil and its meaning leads on to contemplation of God's control over the created universe and the history of humankind and to speculation concerning the End when righteousness will triumph over unrighteousness in God's eternal kingdom. In this process we are introduced to a concept of angelology and demonology which far surpasses anything we find in the pages of the Old Testament and no doubt reflects, in some measure at least, the Hellenistic environment of the time.

One of the most remarkable developments, to which we have only brief reference in the Old Testament, is belief in the resurrection and life after death. This is only part of a very complex eschatological pattern in which writer after writer expresses his hopes and fears concerning 'the last things'. Here we find so much that is familiar to the reader of the New Testament – the idea of the kingdom of God, the 'woes' that will usher in 'the last days', the punishment of the wicked and the reward of the righteous in Sheol (or Hades) and in paradise (or heaven), the final judgment and the great assize, the defeat of Satan and 'the sons of darkness', and so on.

Of particular interest for our understanding of the New Testament background is the belief – or, rather, beliefs – concerning the traditional Messiah (Messiahs) of Jewish expectation and the association of this concept with the figure of the Son of Man.

Such developments during the intertestamental period do not, of course, 'explain' the corresponding New Testament beliefs, far less do they 'explain them away'; but a knowledge of them helps us to enter more fully into the mind of Jesus and his first disciples and to appreciate more fully the origins of the Christian faith.

3. JUDAISM AND JESUS

(a) The Jewishness of Jesus

E. P. Sanders has described Jesus as a recognizable 'eschatological charismatic (Jewish) prophet' who had much more in common with the Judaism of his time than the Gospels seem to indicate (see *Jesus and Judaism*, 1985, pp. 237–41). Whether or not he can be categorized in this or in any other way, it is clear that he lived the life of a Jew, accepted without question the fundamental tenets of the faith handed down from Old Testament times, revered the Sabbath, kept the festivals, shared in the annual pilgrimages, visited the temple, attended the synagogue, shared in its worship wearing the appropriate dress, offered the blessing at meals, observed annual payment to the temple treasury and counselled adherence to certain priestly laws. And in his teaching as well as his practice he was easily recognizable for what he was, for the people addressed him as 'Rabbi' and observed that he spoke as one with authority.

But the Synoptic Gospels make it plain that his relationships with the Pharisees in particular were not all sweetness and light. As the accounts have come down to us, he was most outspoken, even scathing, in his criticism of them, dubs them 'hypocrites' and 'whited sepulchres', calling down imprecations on their heads. They 'shut up the Kingdom of Heaven against men' by denying sinners a share in 'the world to come'. They traverse sea and land to make a single convert and then indoctrinate him to be as hypocritical as they are themselves. They evade even responsibility to parents under cover of the vow *corban* which prevents the transfer of property. They niggle over tithing laws and neglect things that really matter. They quibble over whether the contents of a cup can be ritually clean if the outside of it is deemed to be unclean because touched by 'unclean' hands. They argue over the size of the fringe permitted on their ritual garments and the length of the tassels at each corner. In everything they do they demonstrate that they are true sons of those who killed the prophets.

Attempts have been made to show that such polemics owe more to the theological understanding of the early church than to actual, verifiable history (e.g. E. P. Sanders), or that the criticisms are levelled, not against Pharisees in general, and in particular not against the followers of Hillel (end of first century BC), head of a famous Jewish academy in Jerusalem and an older contemporary of Jesus, with whom he had much in common, but rather against the followers of Shammai, a rival of Hillel, who was much more strict and whose measures deserved the strictures being levelled against them. Whatever qualifications may be given, the Jewishness of Jesus shines through, as does the unique stand he takes to interpret the ancient faith and its promises in the light of his own calling and filial consciousness.

16

(b) Judaism transformed

There has been much debate among scholars concerning Jesus' attitude to Judaism and in particular to its expression in the Law. We have seen that there is a clear continuity between his teaching and that of the Jewish religion in which he was brought up; but there is an equally clear discontinuity which comes out, as we have just seen, in his condemnation of the Pharisees. This discontinuity, however, goes deeper still, for on a number of important issues Jesus took an independent line, bringing to Judaism an interpretation of his own which, in certain cases, effected a radical transformation.

One such issue was the popular notion, advocated by the Zealots, that the expected kingdom would come by military means. By aggression and force of arms the enemies of Israel would be destroyed and a kingdom would be established in which God's people would enjoy political freedom and economic justice alongside religious rights. Jesus uses the same terminology, but reads into it a quite different meaning. The signs of the kingdom are to be found not in killing their enemies, but in loving them; not in hating their persecutors, but in praying for them. The Messiah who will lead them to freedom is not a man of blood with the fire of revolution in his bones, but one who is willing to lay down his life even for his enemies. It is God's kingdom for which they must strive, not their own; and that striving must reveal, not conceal, the true nature of God the Father.

Jesus' expectation of the coming kingdom, it has been argued, had more in common with, say, the Qumran community which envisages a renewed and transformed earth and the appearance of a new heaven and a new earth brought about by the miraculous intervention of God himself (cf. E. P. Sanders, op.cit., pp. 222ff.). But here, too, there is marked discontinuity. In the Dead Sea scrolls, as a result of the final eschatological battle between 'the sons of darkness' and 'the sons of light', Satan and his minions (in heaven and on earth) will be utterly destroyed. To Jesus, however, the object is not to crush those who serve Satan, but rather to set them free from the power of the evil one. Once more, his attitude is determined by his own inner awareness of the nature of God who redeems and saves.

A second issue in which continuity and discontinuity are to be found is in Jesus' understanding of the Law and, within that, his reaction to the 'purity' laws of Judaism. After examining the evidence of the Gospels, E. P. Sanders concludes that 'Jesus did not oppose the Mosaic law, but held it in some ways to be neither adequate nor final' (ibid, p.263). This is well illustrated in his condemnation of lust and hate where the Law speaks of adultery and murder: it is the attitude or intention behind the act and not just the act itself that offends the holy God. It is illustrated, too, in the case of the sabbath as a holy day on which no work should be done: to do good on the sabbath is more praiseworthy in God's sight than the observance of strict sabbath legislation. In other words, personal relationships take precedence over legal rulings. In so judging, Jesus sought not to destroy but to fulfil the law of God.

Observance of 'purity laws' is another case in point. By their very nature they led to an exclusivism and self-justification which were a denial of the free grace of God who sends his rain on the just and the unjust alike. Restoration, not separation, was the will of God for his people. The real defilement does not consist in the breach of rules concerning what can or cannot be done; it is that unaccepting, unloving spirit which denies that love and forgiveness which God shows even towards sinners.

It is just here that the most revolutionary teaching of Jesus shines through: the kingdom of God is open even to sinners who are prepared to follow him in his mission, for it is they – together with the poor, the oppressed, the outcast and the despised – who are the special object of God's love. This is demonstrated not just in his teaching, but also in his life and actions, for he identifies himself with all such, offering them healing and assuring them of the forgiveness of God. In so doing he invites his followers in turn to continue the mission he had begun, warning that, for them as for him, it will involve suffering and even death, but assuring them of the final triumph of God's kingdom and of their place within it as forgiven sinners.

II

Sources and Scripture

I. AN AGE OF LITERARY ACTIVITY

(a) The Septuagint (LXX)

There can be little doubt that the greatest single contribution of Hellenistic culture to early Judaism and the early church was the translation of the Hebrew scriptures into Greek for the use of Greek-speaking Jews in Egypt who were no longer able to read Hebrew and for whom the translations given in the synagogue services had proved inadequate. The translation of the Pentateuch first took place probably during the reign of Ptolemy II (285 – 247 BC), as indicated in the largely legendary tale contained in the Letter of Aristeas (late second century BC), carried out not by a body of learned scribes or 'elders' from Jerusalem who came to a common agreement about it (as suggested in the Letter), but by separate translators in Egypt itself. According to the legend there were seventy-two of these, six from each tribe; but this number was subsequently changed to seventy in the popular mind, perhaps under the influence of the seventy elders who assisted Moses at Sinai or the seventy nations into which, according to Jewish tradition, the Gentiles were divided. In this latter connection, as elsewhere (cf. Luke 10.1,17), variant readings are found indicating seventy and seventy-two. The reading 'seventy' has given to this Greek translation the name 'Septuagint', usually designated by the symbol LXX. The name was subsequently extended to cover not only the Pentateuch but other parts of the Old Testament besides.

As a translation document the Septuagint is not only of considerable interest when read alongside the received Hebrew text; it is also (especially in those parts of it where a rather freer rendering is given) a valuable source for understanding the theological and ethical outlook of Alexandrian Jewry. Its linguistic importance for Christianity centres in the fact that it constitutes a bridge between the Old Testament and the New, the religious vocabulary of New Testament *koine* Greek deriving ultimately not from the Greek as commonly spoken but from the Hebrew world of the Old Testament through the medium of Septuagint Greek. Despite the fact that it was a child of the Hellenistic world, however, the Septuagint's actual contribution as a vehicle of Hellenization was negligible; only certain Greek overtones noticeable here and there would remind its readers of its cultural background. But, of course, as an instrument for the propagation of Judaism and subsequently of Christianity throughout the Dispersion its contribution cannot be over-estimated.

(b) Biblical books

Quite apart from the production of the Septuagint, the Persian and Greek periods witnessed a remarkable output of Jewish literature in both Palestine and the wider Dispersion. In the years following the return from exile a great deal of collating and editing went on, giving shape to what was eventually to be recognized as the Hebrew scriptures. The Psalter and the Book of Proverbs, each of which is 'a collection of collections', would attain their present form around 200 BC and 250 BC respectively. The writer of the Book of Chronicles, about the middle of the fourth century BC, recast the history of his people in keeping with his own priestly convictions and in the light of priestly custom prevalent in his day. Deutero-Zechariah (9–14), some would claim, also reflects the Hellenistic period as do such books as Canticles, Ruth, Ecclesiastes, Esther and Daniel, the last named being more precisely dated around the year 165 BC.

(c) Apocrypha and pseudepigrapha

But these were only a trickle compared with the flood of books that appeared during that time and in subsequent years. Many of them are known to us only by their titles or by brief quotations which appear in later Jewish and, more especially, Christian writings. Valuable information of this kind is given in certain lists or stichometries drawn up in the early Christian centuries to indicate which books were to be accepted as 'canonical' and which were 'extra-canonical' (see further pp. 26ff.). These latter were called by the Rabbis 'outside books' which did not 'defile the hands' (i.e. they did not possess that quality of sacredness which made the handling of them a source of ritual danger). An indication of their identity is given in the Tosefta tractate Yadaim ii, 13 which says, 'The books (*sic*) of Ben Sira and all books which were written from then onwards do not defile the hands.' Lying behind such a judgment was no doubt the popular Jewish belief that inspiration had ceased following the time of Ezra.

Most of these books originated in Palestine and were written in Hebrew or Aramaic; but, with the exception of Ben Sira, they have survived only in Greek and other translations. They became popular with the Greek-speaking Jews of the Dispersion and, in course of time, certain of them were incorporated in the Greek translation of the Hebrew Bible (the Septuagint) which in turn was taken over by the Christian church. These additional books, found in the Greek but not in the Hebrew Old Testament (together with II Esdras and the Prayer of Manasseh which appear in the Latin, Vulgate, version) form what are variously called the Apocrypha (among Protestants) and the Deutero-canonical writings (among Roman Catholics). These are: I Esdras, Tobit, Judith, Additions to Esther, the Wisdom of Solomon, Ecclesiasticus (Ben Sira), I Baruch, the Letter of Jeremiah, the Prayer of Azariah and the Song of the Three Young Men, Susanna, Bel and the Dragon, I and II Maccabees. Apart from Tobit (written before 200 BC) and 2 Esdras (c. AD 100) they all belong to the last two centuries before Christ.

There were many other books, however, not incorporated in the Greek Bible, which were highly valued within the Jewish and later the Christian communities. These and others that followed are generally designated today by the name 'pseudepigrapha' (literally, 'with false superscription'), many of them being written under an assumed name from the past. They are much more difficult to

21

identify and define than the books of the Apocrypha, as is evident from the varying lists that have been produced from time to time. Generally speaking, they are books of Jewish or Jewish-Christian origin (there are also pseudepigrapha of Christian origin) written in Palestine and the wider Dispersion between 200 BC and AD 100 or later which relate to the biblical books and claim to be inspired. As indicated, there is no agreed or 'approved' list of such writings. The best known list for English-speaking readers has been that given by R. H. Charles in 1913 in the second volume of his *Apocrypha and Pseudepigrapha of the Old Testament*. Seventy years or so later this was replaced by two publications which differ considerably from Charles and from each other in the pseudepigrapha listed. In 1984 *The Apocryphal Old Testament* (edited by H. F. D. Sparks) appeared. This purports to be a revision of Charles's second volume dealing with the pseudepigrapha, but in fact omits seven of the books listed there and adds fifteen new ones. In 1983 the first of two volumes, edited by J. H. Charlesworth, appeared under the general title *Old Testament Pseudepigrapha*; together they contain almost three times as many titles as Sparks's book and range over a much broader time-span. Besides those listed in Charles and Sparks as pseudepigrapha Charlesworth names many other cognate writings and indicates that yet others of a similar kind may yet be discovered which will cast further light on early Judaism in the Christian and pre-Christian eras. It is clear that these two more recent publications use different criteria, underlining the fact already stated that there is no generally recognized or 'approved' list of such books.

Such writings, apocryphal and pseudepigraphical alike, show that to many people at that time Judaism was a vibrant but complex religion founded on deep devotion and personal piety (see ch. 5). They reveal a diverse religious community comprised of many religious and political groups and a multitude of people who belonged to no identifiable party at all, held together by one thing above others, their devotion to the Law of God as revealed in scripture and in the laws of their fathers.

(d) Other sources

These lists, however, considerable though they may be, by no means exhaust the source-material for our understanding of the period of early Judaism. Charlesworth indicates nine collections of Jewish or early Christian writings, besides the apocryphal and pseudepigraphical books, which are of importance and deserve the closest study. These are: the Dead Sea Scrolls found at Qumran (c. 150 BC – AD 68); the Jewish writers Philo of Alexandria (c. 20 BC – AD 50) and Josephus (c. AD 37 – AD 100); the rabbinic writings, some of whose traditions pre-date AD 70; the Targums or Aramaic commentaries of scripture; certain magical papyri; the Hermetica (writings of the first few centuries AD attributed to Hermes); the Nag Hammadi (Coptic) codices (first to fourth centuries AD), most of which are gnostic; and the New Testament Apocrypha and Pseudepigrapha which have allusions to early Jewish traditions (cf. Charlesworth, ibid., vol. 1, pp. xxvif.). We shall here glance only briefly at the first three of these.

The discovery of the so-called Dead Sea Scrolls at Qumran in 1948 and in subsequent years brought to light a wealth of material which will go on being deciphered and examined by scholars for many years to come. Many manuscripts have been found and many hundreds of fragments indicating the presence at Qumran, the centre for one branch of the Essene sect during the period 150 BC – AD 68, of a considerable library made up of biblical books and commentaries, apocryphal and pseudepigraphical writings already known to us and other books peculiar to the sect itself having to do with its organization, its beliefs, its religious practice and its hopes for the future.

With the exception of the Book of Esther, every other Old Testament book is represented among the manuscripts or fragments. Popular among the Qumran Covenanters, as they are commonly called, were the Book of Jubilees, of which fragments representing at least ten manuscripts have been found; the Book of Enoch, of which again portions of ten manuscripts have come to light; and several fragments of an Aramaic Testament of Levi and a Hebrew Testament of Naphtali. The interest of the sect in matters apocalyptic is indicated by the fact that fragments of no fewer than seven manuscripts of the Book of Daniel have come to light.

Among the writings peculiar to the sect itself are: the Damascus Document (consisting of admonitions to all who have 'entered the covenant' to remain faithful, and continuing with an indication of the laws governing the community); the Manual of Discipline or Rule of the Community (forming a rule book for the members); the War of the Sons of Light against the Sons of Darkness (describing ceremonial and military plans for the great cosmic battle soon to take place); the Psalms of Thanksgiving (reminiscent of biblical psalms and breathing a spirit of deep devotion); the Genesis Apocryphon (which comments on the Book of Genesis with embellishments of its own and in style has much in common with the Book of Jubilees); and commentaries on the biblical Psalms and the Prophets (e.g. an interesting commentary on Habakkuk) in which the text is interpreted by the writer to apply to the conditions of his own day and the 'sect' to which he belongs (see further pp. 45ff.). Such writings, though limited to the sect of the Essenes at Qumran, are nevertheless of considerable importance for a better understanding of the many-faceted Judaism which prevailed before and at the turn of the Christian era.

The writings of the Jewish philosopher, Philo of Alexandria, and of the Jewish historian Josephus, a high-ranking officer in the Jewish army, were quite prolific and have added enormously to our insights into the Judaism of this period in Egypt and in Palestine. Philo was a contemporary of Jesus and of Paul and in his books had much to say that chimed in with the beliefs of Christianity when in due course it branched out into the Hellenized world. He was an influential man, well educated in Greek philosophy and in the Jewish scriptures, which he knew and revered in their Greek version. He was a staunch Jew who believed that the teachings of the scriptures were in keeping with reason and that their meaning was to be discovered both by reason and by means of mystical interpretation.

He wrote a large number of treatises, many of which we know only by name. They range from a short treatise 'On the Contemplative Life' to a large collection of works entitled 'Exposition of the

Law'; from a series of writings in twenty-one books called 'Allegory of the Jewish Law' to a statement on the theme 'That Every Virtuous Man is Free'. Throughout all these works he showed himself to be a man devoted to his religion and convinced that the Judaism he embraced was the goal of all men's striving, not least in the Hellenized world of Alexandria in which he lived. As an indication, then, of the impact of Hellenism on Judaism at the beginning of the Christian era, Philo occupies an unique place.

Of much greater importance for our understanding of the history of this whole period are the works of the Jewish historian Josephus who, having surrendered to the Roman army against which he had fought, found himself favoured by the Emperor Vespasian and granted the status of a free man. Until the end of the Jewish War with Rome (AD 70) he served as an interpreter and go-between. Thereafter he lived comfortably in Rome with the benefit of a pension and as a Roman citizen.

In these circumstances he was able to devote himself to writing. His first work was *The Jewish War* in seven books; after a quick account of the Hellenistic period as a whole up to the outbreak of the war in AD 66, he devotes the remaining books to an account of the struggle itself and its aftermath. This was followed twenty years later by the *Jewish Antiquities* in twenty books; these cover the entire period from the patriarchs right up to his own day and are designed to show the outstanding achievements of the Jewish people. Attached to this work is his 'Life', an autobiographical work written to defend himself against what he regarded as false accusations. And fourthly, he wrote a fine apologia for Judaism in two volumes, entitled *Against Apion*. Altogether, his works have to be read with care and are not to be taken as either unbiased or objective accounts; nevertheless, they are of the greatest value and stand as our chief source of information concerning the history of the Jews and Judaism from the Hasmonaean period until the fall of Jerusalem in AD 70.

The third source to which allusion is made is 'the rabbinic writings some of whose traditions pre-date AD 70'. This refers particularly to that collection of oral teaching, chiefly dealing with matters of Jewish law, which was systematically classified according to subject-matter and finally put into writing in the form in which we now have it in the Mishnah around the year AD 210. It is divided into six 'orders' and contains in all sixty-three tractates on a whole variety of topics. It represents the judgments and decisions of Rabbis right across the period with which we are dealing as to the right interpretation of the Torah. After the fall of Jerusalem in AD 70 the Rabbis arranged these judgments according to subject-matter rather than according to biblical text. These in turn were elaborated and finally codified in the form in which we now have them (for an English translation see Herbert Danby, *The Mishnah*, 1933). It is not always easy to put a precise date on this judgment and that or to know exactly where in the history of the time to place a named event. But modern scholarship has enabled us to identify with a fair measure of accuracy the source of many pronouncements and traditions, a goodly number of which can safely be traced to the years before the fateful year AD 70.

Besides these and other Jewish sources, there are of course writings from the Greek and Latin world of the times which supplement or correct our knowledge of the Jewish people and their religion. But enough has been said to indicate the prolific output of books of many kinds during these intertestamental years. It remains now to look more closely at those books among them which carried a special degree of sanctity and came to be accepted in an unique way as authoritative in the life of the Jewish people.

2. CANONICITY AND AUTHORITY

It is tolerably easy, given the tools of modern scholarship, to trace the history of the Old Testament books as *literature*, to observe when and by what process they came to be written and what additions or divisions came to be introduced in the course of the years. It is much more difficult to trace the degree of *authority* granted to them or acquired by them with the passing of time. The one concerns the tracing of a literary deposit; the other concerns the tracing of an *idea* or *value-judgment* which is much less easy to pin down.

That *idea* is expressed in the word 'canonicity' which derives from a Greek word *canna*, meaning a reed, then a carpenter's rule, then a standard of assessment and finally a corpus of literature which serves as such a standard and by which other literature can be assessed and judged. The canon of the Old Testament is that body of literature written in Hebrew (and in part in Aramaic) which came to be regarded within Judaism as authoritative in matters of religious faith and practice and was adopted as such by the early Christian church in its Greek translation (the Septuagint), a work which, as we have seen, included some other books besides.

The Old Testament canon is in three parts or three tiers – *Torah* (Law), *Nebi'im* (Prophets: Former and Latter) and *Kethubim* (Writings or Hagiographa) – the first of which was given the greatest esteem in terms of authority, and the last of which remained fluid and undefined right on into the Christian era. In its final form it consisted of twenty-four books which, by a different division, number thirty-nine in the English Versions.

(a) Landmarks in a process

The revealed word of God, in spoken or in written form, when recognized as such, would carry with it the authority of a divine imperative and this would be reinforced when such 'words' came to be collected or recorded in a given document. An early illustration of this is to be found in the Law Book 'discovered' in 621 BC during the reign of Josiah, which is probably to be identified with the central part of our book of Deuteronomy. Another landmark in this process is the recognition by the people of the Law Book read aloud to them by Ezra in 397 BC which some would identify with the Priestly Code and others with the Pentateuch itself. In each case the people listen to words which for them carry the authority of the divine will. Each is a pointer in the direction of what eventually was to be recognized as the canon of the Law.

Another important event in tracing this process of 'canonicity' is the Samaritan schism, brought about around the year 350 BC by the building of a rival temple on Mount Gerizim. The significant point here is that the version of the Law used by the Samaritans is in substantial agreement with the Hebrew version used by the Jews. This strongly suggests that somewhere between 397 BC and 350 BC the corpus of the Torah must have been completed, since it is most unlikely that it would have been the same for both Samaritans and Jews if it had been compiled *following* the schism. It is obvious that in succeeding years the Torah continued to be revered by the people and to have its authority more firmly established, particularly as Judaism developed a more legalistic interpretation of divine revelation (see pp. 60ff.) and as the focus of attention moved from the temple to the Torah, a process which is most noticeable during the period 300 – 200 BC. Be that as it may, the Book of Tobit, for example, written before the year 200 BC, confirms by the respect it shows for the Law that by that time the Torah had assumed truly canonical authority. This impression is reinforced by Ben Sira, writing about 180 BC, who identifies the Law with Wisdom, whose praise he extols (24.23,25).

Alongside this process of recognition, resulting in the assumption of the canonical authority of the Torah, went that of the Former and Latter Prophets. From early times cycles of tradition were preserved, edited and combined – a process which was given greater impetus under the influence of Ezra's Law Book; the fact that these traditions and their editing went beyond the Torah into what came to be called the Former Prophets (Joshua, Judges, Samuel, Kings) underlined the authority of such works. From early times, too, the spoken words of the prophets, uttering their 'Thus saith the Lord', carried their own weight of authority. This was perpetuated and enhanced by their compilation and editing in written form.

In terms of 'canonicity', however, we again look to the turn of the second century BC for a clear landmark. This is given once more by Ben Sira (*c*. 180 BC), who indicates his familiarity with the Law and the Prophets more or less as we have them today. His references to people and events show a knowledge of both the Former Prophets and the three major prophets Isaiah, Jeremiah and Ezekiel; more significantly still, he alludes to 'the twelve (minor) prophets' as a distinct collection (cf. 49.10).

The conclusion we must draw is that by this time the prophetic writings formed a closed *corpus* of writings which carried canonical authority. This would explain why the Book of Daniel, for example, did not appear in the prophetic canon even though it might be regarded as a 'prophetic' book. The reason is that Daniel did not in fact appear until some years after Ben Sira's work (c. 165 BC). It is of interest to note that Daniel itself refers to the Book of Jeremiah as authoritative 'scripture' (9.2). The cumulative evidence points to the assumption that by this time the Prophets were credited with canonical authority. One factor facilitating this process may have been the prevalent belief that from the time of Ezra onwards, prophetic inspiration had ceased and prophecy itself was deemed to be dumb (cf. I Maccabees 4.46; 9.27; 14.41; Psalm 74.9; *Against Apion* I.8; *Antiquities* XI. vi. 1). Despite this belief, however, prophecy as we know did continue, and prophetic oracles have been preserved and incorporated in the prophetic corpus, either as separate books or as 'interpolations' in the writings of other canonical prophets (cf. Zechariah 9–14; Isaiah 24–27).

But clearer still is the testimony of Ben Sira's grandson who, about 132 BC, translated his grandfather's book into Greek and added to it his own prologue. There he speaks of 'the Law and the Prophets and the others that followed them', 'the Law and the Prophets and the other books of our fathers', and 'the Law itself, the Prophecies and the rest of the books'. He thus confirms the canonicity of the first two divisions, but indicates a third collection of books whose scope and number are still fluid and not yet recognized by any particular name.

The evidence of the New Testament is open to different interpretations. There Jesus states: 'Everything written about me in the law of Moses and the prophets and the psalms must be fulfilled' (Luke 24.44). This reference to 'the psalms' may indicate that the third section of the canon, to be called 'the Writings', was as yet undefined. On the other hand, it may stand for the whole collection of writings, being the first and most important part of it, or the reference may be to the use of these three scripture sections in the synagogue worship.

Further evidence is given by the writer of II Esdras (c. AD 100), who refers to twenty-four 'canonical' books (14.44ff.) which, by a different division, appear as thirty-nine in our versions, and by Josephus, who gives the number as twenty-two, which no doubt represent a different grouping of the twenty-four already alluded to. The conclusion we may legitimately draw from this accumulated evidence is that by New Testament times the canon of scripture as we know it was virtually closed, although as yet the expression 'the Writings' had not been used of the third section of it. The use of the word 'virtually' in this connection is required for at least two reasons. One is that three Old Testament books, which are not quoted at all in the New Testament, remained controversial among the Jews for some time. These were Esther, the Song of Songs and Ecclesiastes, the last two of which were a bone of contention between the schools of Hillel and Shammai. Even after the Council of Jamnia in AD 90, whose importance in the codification of the canon is hotly debated by scholars, these three writings remained uncertain. The second reason is that the New Testament refers to certain writings, not generally regarded by us today as 'canonical', in such a way as to suggest that there was in fact no clear line of demarcation between these and other books to be found in what came to be known as 'the Writings'. The clearest illustration of this is in Jude 14 – 16, where reference is made to the Book of Enoch as if it were authoritative scripture. It is of interest to note in this connection that a fragment containing 1 Enoch 1.9 (the passage alluded to) has been found in Aramaic in one of the caves containing the Dead Sea Scrolls. Again, in Jude 9 there is an allusion to the dispute between the Devil and the archangel Michael over the body of Moses which may refer to a lost Jewish writing, The Assumption of Moses, known to us from quotations in other writers. Hebrews 11.35, with its reference to resurrection, probably has in mind the martyrdom of Eleazar and the Seven Brothers recorded in II Maccabees 6–7. The words of Paul in I Corinthians 2.9 ('Things which eye saw not', etc.), Origen and others contrary to what say do not come from the so-called Apocalypse (or Prophecy or Mysteries) of Elijah.

This fluidity of 'authoritative scripture' in 'the Writings' is not surprising when we bear in mind the fact that the Greek version (the Septuagint) of the scriptures, which was the version used by the early church, was wider in scope and contained material not to be found in the Hebrew text.

(b) Hebrew and Greek versions

Reference has already been made to the legend contained in the Letter of Aristeas that the Septuagint was the work of seventy-two 'elders' in Egypt in the time of Ptolemy II. The truth behind this story, as we have seen, is no doubt that the Septuagint translation emerged in Alexandria, the greatest literary centre of the ancient world, as a Greek Targum (translation/paraphrase) for the benefit of those Jews who were unable to understand the Hebrew scriptures. It is clear that 'the Law' and 'the Prophets' were available in the Greek text well before the Christian era, say about 250 BC and 150 BC respectively. It is less clear, however, when the translation of 'the Writings' book place, what Ben Sira's grandson calls 'the rest of the books', or at what point they came to be accepted as canonical scripture. In pre-Christian times there was no agreed list of those books which, in the Greek translation, included a number not to be found in the Hebrew version. It is these additional books, as already noted, which for the most part make up what we know as the Apocrypha. We have already observed that during this period when the 'canon' of scripture remained 'ragged at the edges' numbers of 'pseudepigraphical' writings were also produced which some Jews and Christians at least regarded as inspired and so authoritative. Such books were not regarded as 'canonical' in the sense that the Law and the Prophets were. But it is equally wrong to describe them as 'non-canonical'; indeed, to apply the word 'canon' positively or negatively to 'the rest of the books' *at this period* is to adopt a historically inappropriate and indeed inaccurate concept. In other words, it is wrong to speak about a 'Greek canon' which can be set over against a different 'Hebrew canon'. There was in fact only one canon, that of the Hebrew Bible.

(c) The worth of scripture

It is altogether unsatisfactory to try to explain the fact of 'canonicity' by reference to some purely mechanical idea, for example that inspiration was believed to have ceased at the time of Ezra or that only those books originally written in Hebrew could be acceptable. It is equally unsatisfactory to look to, say, the Council of Jamnia in

AD 90 as the determinative factor in any such process of recognition. The only adequate explanation is the recognition on the part of the Jewish people as a whole over a long period of time of the intrinsic worth of this body of literature which enshrined the story of God's dealings with their forefathers and their nation as no other literature was able to do. It told them about the nature of the God who had chosen to reveal himself to them as he had done to no other nation and about that God's choice of them to be his special people.

The recognition of this 'intrinsic worth' became clearer as the scribes, following the example of Ezra, gave themselves to a study of the Law, seeking an interpretation of its meaning and applying its laws and regulations to the changed and changing circumstances of the days in which they lived. The development of the synagogues and their book-centred worship of God added very considerably to the worth of the scriptures in their eyes. This in turn bred or encouraged a deep personal piety among many who found the sacred writings both inspired by God and authoritative for their own life and conduct. So it was that, some time before the outbreak of the Maccabaean Revolt in 167 BC a subtle transfer of emphasis had taken place from temple to Torah so that by then and in subsequent years the Jews could aptly be described as 'the people of the Book'.

To the Christian church the scriptures were equally inspired and equally authoritative. But there was one big difference. They pointed beyond themselves for their fulfilment; and that fulfilment was to be found in the story of Jesus of Nazareth who was the Christ, the Son of God. The story of the Hebrew scriptures was one of promise and fulfilment. It gave the promise of a Saviour who would deliver his people; of the saved people of Israel who would become the saving people of God; of the ultimate fulfilment of God's purpose for Jew and Gentile in the establishment of his eternal kingdom; but nowhere was this realized except in vision and dream. In Jesus, however, they saw the ancient promise of a Saviour actually fulfilled: in the church, the new Israel, they saw the true expression of God's own covenant people; and in Christ's resurrection and parousia they recognized his kingdom coming with power.

32

They saw the Hebrew scriptures as a book incomplete in itself at the close of which were written the words 'to be continued'. There must have been many in Israel who, like Saul of Tarsus, were puzzled and frustrated. The ancient promises were surely of God; but little was said about the how and where and when. But in Christ they saw these things fulfilled in the sense that he gave them new and relevant meaning. And so in course of time in the New Testament record the church found the key to the Old. The two were bound together in one in terms of promise and fulfilment as the sacred scriptures of the church.

III

Biblical Interpretation in Early Judaism and the New Testament

The Jewish people have been described as 'the people of the Book'; but they might equally well be described as 'the people of biblical exegesis'. This is true in a particular way of the years between the time of Ezra the scribe and, say, the end of the second century AD, for these centuries witnessed a time of intensive – and extensive – exegetical activity. The process was in many ways a legitimate continuation of what had already begun within the Old Testament itself and found expression in the New. It owed much to the synagogues, as houses of study and prayer, and also to the 'schools' of 'the wise' where meticulous attention was paid to the scriptures and their application to the life and circumstances of the times and to the central place given to the study of these scriptures by the Pharisees and other religious 'parties' within the people.

I. INTERPRETATION IN THE OLD TESTAMENT

(a) *Event and interpretation*

The interpretation of scripture began long before the closure of the canon and belongs to the very nature of scripture itself. The later compilers and editors of the Old Testament text would surely have agreed with the subsequent comment in the Talmud where the question is asked, 'What is Torah?', and the answer is given, 'The interpretation of Torah'. Event and interpretation of event belong inseparably together as vehicles of divine revelation. Different interpretations of the same event are given in the light of the prevailing circumstances or the religious outlook of the writer concerned. A case in point is that of the Exodus theme which keeps on appearing in book after book in new forms in succeeding generations, not least in the context of the return from exile. The Deuteronomists, moreover, clearly re-interpreted historical events on the basis of the one central Jerusalem temple and the idolatrous nature of local shrines; the priestly writers supplied their own interpretations and accounts in the light of divine revelation as they understood it; the prophets gave their own interpretation to existing traditions (e.g. Jacob in Hosea 12) and had their own prophetic material used (e.g. Amos and Hosea) by prophetic groups in Judah or by the Deuteronomists.

Commenting on the authors of the priestly source (P), R. H. Pfeiffer says; they 'did not hesitate to re-write their sources, entirely removing whatever conflicted with their theories and adding whatever was needed to integrate their work' (*Introduction to the Old Testament*, 1948, pp.206f.). This marked degree of freedom in re-interpreting a given source within a new context is illustrated in P's account of the story of creation. The meaning of the story is more important to the writer than the words or concepts used to express it and so details of this kind can be readily changed to make clear the revelation conveyed.

Another example of re-interpretation on the part of the priestly writers is to be found in the work of the Chronicler which may be described as an interpretation or *midrash* on the historical books of Samuel and Kings. The Chronicler is not afraid to make use of modifications, adaptations and extensions of the primary sense of his text for the purpose of supporting the authoritative teaching of his own day or the accepted ritualistic practice prevailing in the circle to which he himself belonged. Indeed he goes further than this and is much more drastic than the later Rabbis (who had a fixed text in front of them) in his dealing, e.g., with conflicting accounts in the scriptures or with discrepancies in parallel or associated texts. In I Samuel 17, for example, the giant Goliath is slain by David, but in II Samuel 21 the deed is said to have been performed by a certain Elhanan. In re-writing the latter text the Chronicler (I Chronicles 20.5) quite simply sets matters right by declaring that the one whom Elhanan slew was not Goliath at all, but Goliath's brother. Later rabbinic expositors would have done this kind of thing by way of added commentary; but the Chronicler has no qualms about changing the text itself.

(b) Levites as interpreters of Torah

A significant passage for our understanding of the development of this process of interpretation is II Chronicles 17.9, in which the writer refers to the appointment of certain priests and Levites as itinerant preachers who toured the country, teaching the people the meaning of Torah: 'And they taught in Judah, having the book of the Law of the Lord with them; they went about through all the cities of Judah and taught among the people.' This situation no doubt reflects the practice of the Chronicler's own day and indicates that at that time the priests and Levites were actively engaged in the task of expounding and interpreting the word of God to the common people. Without hesitation he refers this situation back to the time of Jehoshaphat and so claims for this institution a place in antiquity and in the revealed will of God.

Elsewhere in Chronicles these same Levites are presented as singers and musicians who are not only good at the mechanical performance of their duties, but are said to be 'skilled' in the sense of understanding what they are doing. In II Chronicles 30.22 they are given the name 'maskilim', a word which occurs several times in Daniel, for example, to signify men who are specially endowed with divine wisdom to instruct others, and again (with the same reference) in the headings of a number of the Psalms. The picture thus emerges of the Levites of the third and fourth centuries BC and earlier functioning, not only as those who offer sacrifices, but also as preachers of God's word and as instructors in the Torah.

2. RABBINIC INTERPRETATION

(a) Ezra, the Sopherim and their successors

This function is, of course, associated with the name of Ezra, the priest-scribe, who is described in scripture as 'a ready scribe in the Law of Moses' (Ezra 7.6), who 'set his heart to seek the law of the

Lord and do it' (Ezra 7.10). Elsewhere (in Neh. 8.8) it is said that he 'read the book, the law of God, distinctly' and 'gave the sense so that they understood the meaning'. The word translated 'distinctly' means literally 'explaining' or 'separating', i.e. separating the words from one another so as to give the clear meaning, whilst the root of the word translated 'seek' is used frequently in post-biblical Hebrew to signifiy an exposition or commentary. Ezra is thus regarded – with some justification – as the father of Jewish exegesis who was inspired by God in the way that Moses himself had been inspired to make known the Torah on Mount Sinai. Ezra and his successors, the Sopherim, it was believed, took over the religious heritage of Moses and the prophets and laid the foundation for all future developments.

In the years following the promulgation of the Law by Ezra the need must have been felt for both definition and interpretation, for it was not always self-evident what exactly constituted the law of God, nor was it at all clear how particular laws were to be applied in every day life and affairs. And so the Sopherim, in succession to Ezra the scribe, set themselves to meet this need by collecting, preserving, interpreting and teaching the Law. As a result it is chiefly due to them that, before the end of the Persian period, the Pentateuch came to be recognized as canonical scripture. No doubt we are to see in these men and their successors the historical reality behind what Jewish tradition knows as the 'Men of the Great Synagogue', whose founder and first president was said to be Ezra himself.

Shortly after the beginning of the Greek period the influence of the priestly scribes was replaced by that of another class of scribes, chiefly lay, who applied themselves diligently to the task of interpreting and applying the Law in the light of the changed circumstances of their day. This group of men in due course appeared as the party of the Pharisees whose authority in the Supreme Council of the Jews, to be known subsequently as the Sanhedrin, was second only to that of the high priest and his family. These teachers laid great stress on the importance of tradition in their exposition of the scriptures and frequent reference is made throughout the rabbinic literature to the statements and judgments of the great Rabbis who had gone before. In the Mishnah tractate Pirke' Abot (1.2 ff.) it is claimed that the tradition of the Sopherim (who had succeeded the great Ezra himself) had been passed on by Simon the Just to one Antigonus of Socho and that thereafter it was transmitted to a series of teachers whose names are given in pairs right down in line of succession to Hillel and Shammai in the time of Jesus.

(b) Mishnah and Midrash: oral tradition

The rabbinic sources, in which this oral tradition had been handed down and which remained oral throughout the intertestamental period, are of two kinds, known as *Mishnah* and *Midrash*, which represent two forms or methods of exegesis. They differ from each other in a number of respects, but chiefly in that the Mishnaic approach is a systematic and topical classification of the discussion and decisions of the Rabbis without any particular rooting in the text of scripture, whereas the Midrashic approach is closely bound up with scripture and is an exposition of its revealed laws and precepts.

Here we look at the midrashic method, since it relates closely to that development of interpretation we have already observed in the Old Testament itself. It consists of a sort of running commentary on the text of scripture in which the particular lesson or precept, which the teacher wished to impart, was found in and expounded from a particular passage. It is called 'Midrash', from the root *d-r-sh* meaning 'to seek', because it is a process of seeking out or enquiring into the written text to discover its implications. Such *Midrash* is in two parts or assumes two forms. The first is called *Halakah* (from the root *h-l-k* meaning 'to walk'), which consists of regulations concerning matters of civil and religious law. It shows the way a man should walk by making clear how he should obey the Law in every detail; i.e., it is an exegesis of biblical laws out of which come authoritative regulations for the proper ordering of life. The second is called *Haggadah* (from the root *n-g-d*, meaning 'to tell' or 'to recount'). This is part of the rabbinic literature which is a development of the biblical stories rather than the biblical laws, an exposition of belief and doctrine rather than of precept and ordinance.

In some sense this midrashic method of interpretation is a natural development of the method adopted by the priestly writer (P) and by the Chronicler, with this difference, that, whereas the biblical writer was able to incorporate his interpretation in the text of scripture itself, the later Jewish interpreter, with the fixed text of the Torah or the Prophets before him, had to be content with a separate midrashic comment on the text. But in principle this method was a continuation of that already adopted by the biblical writers themselves.

As an example of this approach we may take the Midrash on Gen. 42, which gives the account of the ten brothers of Joseph going to Egypt to buy corn. This is used to substantiate the claim that a quorum for public prayer should be ten men. It finds support in the fact that elsewhere (in the story of the ten spies in Numbers 14.27) the number 'ten' is used in close association with the word 'congregation' and so a congregation consists of ten men. Or again, we may take the Midrash on Gen. 1.1 which begins with the expression *bereshit* meaning 'in the beginning'. The fact that the Bible thus begins with the letter *beth* raises all sorts of questions. For example, it is asked, 'Why was the world created with a *beth*?' One answer is, 'To teach that there are two worlds' (the letter *beth* having the numerical value of 'two'). Another is, 'Because it connotes "blessing" ' (*beth* being the first letter of *berachah*, meaning 'blessing'). A third is, 'Because it has two projecting points, one pointing upwards to God the Creator and one pointing backwards to the God who has led his people.'

(c) Forms of rabbinic exegesis

Being a revelation of religion (see below), the scriptures embody revelation in their every part, every jot and tittle of which is of significance for the purpose of deductional exegesis. To the exegetes every word and every phrase is of the utmost importance and has its part to play in the divine disclosure. In this way there arose a form of exegesis very different from that of the modern exegete with his ideas of historical development and literary criticism. 'This conception of Scripture,' writes G. F. Moore, 'leads to an atomistic exegesis, which interprets sentences, clauses, phrases and even single words, independently of the context or the historical occasion, as divine oracles; combines them with other similarly detached utterances, and makes large use of analogy of expression, often by purely verbal association' (*Judaism*, vol. I, 1927, p. 248). This approach meant that the interpretation of scripture was often forced and fanciful.

In due course the attempt was made in rabbinic circles to bring order out of chaos and to establish certain rules for the proper ordering of scriptural exegesis. Rabbi Hillel (*c*. 10 BC) for example, expressed the principles of interpretation current in his circle in the form of seven well-defined rules which had as their basis the assumption that scripture should, for the most part, be interpreted by scripture – by inference or by analogy or by deduction and so forth. About a century later these were expanded to thirteen by Rabbi Ishmael and much later still, in the second century AD, to thirty-two by Rabbi Eliezer ben Joses. J. Bonsirven sums up the rabbinic methods of exegesis under four main headings (cf. *Exégèse Rabbinique et Exégèse Paulinienne*, 1938, chs. 2–5):

1. The simple or direct understanding of the text without resort to cunningly devised 'rules' or *middot* as they are called in Hebrew.
2. The dialectical method of Hillel and the rest.
3. Philological exegesis with its examination of grammatical and syntactical niceties.
4. The allegorical or symbolic, sometimes like, but more often quite unlike, that of Hellenistic exegesis.

(d) Scripture and revelation

The Rabbis believed that the scriptures were throughout a revelation of religion in the widest sense of that word, because in and through them he had chosen to make known his character and ways and what he requires of men in their relations to him and to one another. Such revelation was made known not only through the inspired text of scripture, but also through the inspired application of mind and heart to the text in deducing what is implied but not explicitly stated there. In terms of revelation, then, the text and the interpretation of it belong inseparably together. There could not be two Laws, one written and one oral, but one Law in two texts which together contained the sum of divine revelation.

Each part was not only of divine origin; it was also of equal antiquity and authority, having been given by God through Moses at Sinai. Historically the development of the oral law could be traced, in large part at least, to the pronouncements of particular Rabbis. But that did not nullify the fact that those Rabbis, in whatever age they taught, stood in and represented a tradition which had already been known by God. As F. F. Bruce puts it: '*Historically*, the oral law is a practical commentary on the written law, growing over the centuries as the written rulings and statutes were adapted and applied to the changing conditions of life in succeeding generations. *Dogmatically*, however, the oral law, quite recent as it might be, was invested with authority by being promulgated as "Mosaic Torah from Sinai" ' (*Tradition Old and New*, 1970, p. 22).

As the revelation of religion, moreover, it was believed that the scriptures could not contradict themselves and so it was the responsibility of the exegete to defend the self-authentication of scripture and to show that any differences which might appear were more apparent than real. The difficulties of such a task are hinted at in a story concerning Hananiah ben Hezekiah, a prominent member of the school of Shammai who sat up night after night 'burning the midnight oil' (the story says he used up no less than 300 jars of it!) trying to make the Book of Ezekiel agree with the Pentateuch. At long last he was able to offer an exegesis which harmonized every detail and removed every apparent contradiction between these two parts of scripture.

Despite the assurances of this story, however, many difficulties of scriptural interpretation remained, and the hope is again and again expressed that in the messianic age the obscurities to be found in the Torah would be fully explained. In that great day, God himself would give a new interpretation of scripture and disclose to all his people the secrets of his will. Until that day dawned, it was the supreme duty of every Jew so to study the inspired Torah with its sacred tradition that he might the better co-operate with

41

God in hastening the appearance of the messianic kingdom and the world to come.

But just as Moses was the source of all law-giving, so, it was believed, was he the source of all prophecy. 'The revelation to Moses was complete and final; no other prophet should ever make any innovation in the law. The forty-eight prophets and seven prophetesses who came after him neither took away anything that was written in the Law nor added anything to it. . . Moses is the fountain-head of prophecy in so literal a sense that it is said that he uttered all the words of the prophets besides his own' (G. F. Moore, *Judaism*, vol. 1, 1927, p. 239). It is significant that in the tradition recorded in the tractate Pirke' Abot the prophets are given an important place in the unbroken line of transmission of the Law from Moses to succeeding generations (cf. 1.1). There was thus a very close relationship between the Law and the prophets. Just as the great prophets had sought to expound and apply the teachings of Moses, so Ezra ('the second Moses') and his successors in the long tradition, in expounding and applying the Law, believed they were interpreting to their generation the teachings of the prophets.

3. INTERPRETATION IN OTHER TYPES OF JEWISH LITERATURE

Quite apart from the Greek (Septuagint) translation of the Old Testament with its variant readings and 'interpretative' renderings, there is quite diverse Jewish literature which is of considerable interest, illustrating as it does the varying types of interpretation of scripture prevalent at this time.

(a) The Genesis Apocryphon and Jubilees

One example is the Genesis Apocryphon from Qumran which deals with the story of Abraham contained in Genesis 12 and 13, and is the earliest extant post-biblical midrash known to us. It takes the form of a running commentary on the biblical account, following the biblical text quite closely, but supplying rich and colourful haggadic (story) amplifications. The author tries to make the biblical story more attractive, more edifying and more intelligible by filling in geographical data, for example, or by expounding obscure references. He tries, too, to reconcile any apparently conflicting statements so as to allay doubts on the part of the readers and deliberately omits any reference which might be an offence to pious ears. Geza Vermes sees in this writing the lost link between the biblical and the rabbinic midrash and points to others of a somewhat similar character already known to us.

The most significant of these is the book of Jubilees, which is a midrashic commentary on Genesis and part of Exodus, purporting to be a revelation given by God to Moses on Mount Sinai. In content and emphasis it is closely related to the Genesis Apocryphon, with which the author of Jubilees was familiar, and shows a greater apologetic subtlety than its predecessor and a greater doctrinal bias.

(b) Targumim

Somewhat the same expansion of the biblical text under the influence of doctrinal beliefs can be illustrated also from the Targumim or paraphrases in Aramaic of the passages from the Law and the Prophets set for reading in the synagogue worship. Their later recensions available to us no doubt reflect fairly accurately the oral material of pre-Christian times. One of the most interesting is the Targum on Isaiah 53 where the Suffering Servant is identified with the Messiah, but the interpretation given to the whole chapter is radically different from the original intention of the Old Testament prophet. The Messiah here presented is the Messiah of David who will triumph over the heathen; the suffering he is to endure is reduced to the barest minimum and is completely devoid of the vicarious quality which we find in the biblical passage. Indeed, the sufferings undergone by the Servant in the biblical passage are transferred one after another to the enemies of Israel and are brought about by the victory of the Messiah. In this way the biblical passage is re-written – as in the case of the Genesis Apocryphon and Jubilees – in this case with the sole objective of giving prominence to the Davidic Messiah.

(c) Apocalyptic books

Of importance, too, is the body of apocalyptic literature, produced for the most part during the period 200 BC – AD 100, with its own peculiar insights and emphases. These books were written in the name of certain great men of the past by unknown scribes who believed that they too stood in a long line of tradition going back to the one in whose name they wrote. Thus, in the Book of Jubilees, to which reference has already been made, the apocalyptic tradition in which the writer stands, together with the Torah itself, is apparently to be traced back to Moses at Sinai (cf. 1.27; 6.22, etc.). Again, in II Esdras 14, Ezra 'the second Moses' receives from God the twenty-four books of canonical scripture which he has to publish openly and the seventy books of the apocalyptic tradition which he has to keep secret until the appointed time when he would 'deliver them to the wise among thy people' (14.46).

As with the rabbinic scribes, so with these writers, the Torah was authoritative scripture; but it was to the prophets especially that they looked for a message from God for the tortuous times in which they were then living, and more particularly to the predictive side of prophecy.

Indeed, apocalyptic may be said to be the child of prophecy in the sense that it continues the message of the prophets by interpreting it and re-interpreting it in the light of the changed circumstances of the apocalyptists' own day.

These ancient prophecies, it was firmly believed, were to be read in terms of 'the end' and were to be interpreted and re-interpreted so as to fit into the great final drama of God's triumph over all his foes. Here again the apocalyptists were being true to the tradition of the Old Testament itself, much of which is written in terms of promise and fulfilment. General prophetic promises now become precise apocalyptic assurances. In answer to the prophets' cry, 'How long, O Lord, how long?', the apocalyptists gave the year, the day and the hour. Their method was to scrutinize the writings of the prophets for clues concerning the future destiny of Israel and the nations and in particular for unfulfilled predictions which were capable of ingenious exegesis. Not only did they interpret prophecy

44

– as for example the seventy years' captivity in Jeremiah which became seventy weeks of years in Daniel – they were also prepared to re-interpret previous interpretations – as in the Testaments of the XII Patriarchs and elsewhere where Daniel's seventy weeks of years are themselves given yet another interpretation.

These prophecies, they believed, had a secret or hidden meaning whose interpretation had been intentionally concealed by God till the last days. These last days were now at hand and God had at last revealed his secrets to his saints who were bidden to record them in their books, that the wise among the people might read and understand.

Their adoption of pseudonymity lent power to their utterances, the story of the past (with its accurate so-called 'predictions' of historical events) making more graphic and dramatic their message for the present time and inspiring in their readers a more confident hope in the speedy fulfilment of God's purposes.

In their interpretation of Old Testament prophecy, moreover, they drew freely upon non-biblical tradition as well as biblical, making free use of cosmic mythology with its profuse symbolism. In particular they were fascinated by chronology and numerology, juggling with figures in an attempt to predict the time of the coming kingdom. By means of what we might call 'allegorical arithmetic' they played around with figures and cycles and number patterns in an attempt to pin-point the fulfilment of each elusive unfulfilled prophecy, like the three and a half years of tribulation in Daniel which is re-interpreted as 1,150 days and then as 1,290 days, and finally as 1,335 days (cf. Daniel 12.5–13). This is a clear case of prediction being reviewed and recast by later hands in the light of the apparent failure of earlier attempts to indicate the time of the End. It is small wonder that such writers were referred to disparagingly by the Rabbis of a later generation as 'calculators of the end'.

(d) Qumran literature

The study and interpretation of the Law and the Prophets was an imperative duty of every member of the Qumran community whose leader, the Teacher of Righteousness, was believed to be specially gifted by God for the task of exposition. Their familiarity with the text of scripture is demonstrated in the number of direct quotations to be found in the scrolls and by anthologies of Old Testament words and phrases which provide an 'implicit exegesis'.

More significant than these, however, is the use made of a type of *midrash* on a portion of scripture (more especially prophetic scripture) which follows up the text with a particular kind of interpretation or *pesher*, as it is called. The best known and most complete of these is the *pesher* on the first two chapters of Habakkuk in which a verse-by-verse or section-by-section commentary is given. The original prophecy, it is believed, was a mystery (*raz*) even to the prophet himself. Its meaning had remained sealed, but now its interpretation had been made known. To the Teacher of Righteousness 'God (had) made known all the mysteries of the words (spoken by) his servants the prophets'.

At the risk of oversimplification we may say that the form of interpretation here adopted follows three lines of application. These may be summed up in the words 'contemporization', 'accommodation' and 'allegorization'.

In the first of these the interpretation makes plain that the prophetic text applies not to the time in which the prophet himself lived and spoke, but rather to the contemporary situation of the sect (or to some event in the history of that sect) to which the Teacher of Righteousness belonged. It is not simply that what is now happening can be *likened* to what was spoken of in the prophet's day. It is something much more radical than that. What the Teacher of Righteousness is giving is not just a re-interpretation of prophecy, but the *real* and *only* interpretation – the word given to the prophet by God but which had remained a mystery to him and to all who followed him until the Teacher arose who was able, by the help of God, to reveal its secret.

This contemporary situation, about which the ancient prophecies spoke, was of supreme importance for one very good reason – it marked the beginning of the end! The message of the prophets was in fact a message about the end-time which was about to be ushered in.

In the interest of this interpretation the prophetic text is subjected to a minute examination in which every phrase and almost every word is made to apply to this new historical situation or to the time of the end, quite regardless of the historical setting of the passage in its original context. In Deuteronomy 32.33, for instance, reference is made to the wicked whose 'wine is the venom of dragons, the pitiless poison of cobras'. In the interpretation these dragons are identified with the kings of the nations, and the poison of cobras is the 'chief of the kings of Greece'. Or again, in Numbers 24.14 the words 'a star comes forth from Jacob and a sceptre rises from Israel' are made to apply to *two* important messianic figures in the hopes of the Qumran community itself. This is got by a certain forcing of words to fit in with the sect's own eschatological expectations, for although a single messianic figure was originally intended under the signs of 'star' and 'sceptre', they are represented as standing for two distinct people.

The second line of interpretation is closely associated with the first. We might describe it by the word 'accommodation'. Here the Old Testament text is not only wrested from its original context, it is at the same time considerably modified and even deliberately changed – by means of different or variant readings – so as to adapt it to a new situation or make it serve a new purpose. Thus in Ezekiel 44.15 we are told that the Lord will be served by 'the levitical priests, sons of Zadok', that is, by one particular class of people. In the Damascus Document the conjunction 'and' is inserted twice over to make the verse indicate *three* groups of people corresponding to three groups within the community itself – 'the priests *and* the Levites *and* the sons of Zadok who have kept charge of my sanctuary'. That is, we have here a deliberate manipulation of the text to suit the purpose which the interpreter had in mind.

The third line of interpretation is that of allegorization. The Qumran Covenanters were not, of course, pioneers in this usage. From at least as early as the sixth century BC it is found among the Greeks as a method of interpreting the works of Homer and was popular among the Stoics. In the first half of the second century BC the Jew Aristobulus, about whom we know very little, apparently applied Stoic allegorical methods to his exposition of the Old Testament, and subsequently the method of allegorical interpretation is found in such books as the Letter of Aristeas, IV Maccabees, the Book of Wisdom and the rabbinic literature generally as well as the writings of Philo.

Writing of the rabbinic exegetes, J. Bonsirven says they 'do not distinguish in scripture a body and soul, a literal sense and a spiritual sense (that is, after the style of traditional Greek allegorists). They discern in Holy Scripture only a unique meaning and content. . . the art of the exegete consists in bringing out these significances with the aid either of subtle comparisons, or of ingenious interpretation or of exegetical tradition' (*Exégèse Rabbinique et Exégèse Paulinienne*, 1938, pp. 250f.). This judgment applies equally well to the Qumran exegetes. In the Damascus Document, for instance, an interpretation is given of Numbers 21.17f., which tells of 'the well which the princes dug, which the nobles of the people delved, with the sceptre and with staves'. The well, says the commentator, is the Law; the diggers are those Israelites who repented and sojourned in the land of Damascus; the sceptre or staff is the Expounder of the Law; the nobles of the people are those who have come to dig the well with the staves. In such ways as this, the secret word of scripture was made known and was seen to apply in its every detail to that great climax of history in which the Qumran Covenanters were at that very time living.

4. INTERPRETATION IN THE NEW TESTAMENT

It is against this background of Jewish interpretation that we are to understand some at least of the principles of biblical exegesis contained in the New Testament scriptures. As we shall see, there are traces there of exegetical method familiar to us from the records of rabbinic jurisprudence, although the similarities are more striking with the methods and approach to be found in the Qumran texts.

(a) Familiarity with the Old Testament

One of the first things to strike us about the New Testament writers is their *familiarity* with the Old Testament scriptures. This is hardly surprising, of course, because most of them were themselves Jews who, as children of their time, had grown up under the influence of the synagogue and the schools. Again and again quotations are given from the Old Testament, sometimes from the Hebrew text and at other times in the Septuagint form. Certainly, the Old Testament was known to them as a written book as is evidenced by such phrases as 'for it is written', or 'as it is written'. Such phrases remind us of the rabbinic use of *Katub*, 'that which is written'. Elsewhere an Old Testament passage is introduced simply by the word 'saying' which recalls the common Hebrew expression, 'as it is said'.

But perhaps more significant, because more frequent, than direct quotations are those compositions, already noted in connection with the Qumran writings, in which Old Testament expressions are collected together to form an anthology, thus providing what we might call 'an implicit exegesis'. This is familiar to us in the New Testament Apocalypse which, though it contains no direct Old Testament quotation, nevertheless teems with Old Testament allusions. Another good example is Stephen's speech in Acts 7, where a whole span of Old Testament history is summarized and interpreted in relation to Jesus Christ. In certain places, as in Mark 15.24, the Old Testament material is so closely woven into the narrative that the reader who is unfamiliar with the Old Testament passage involved would hardly guess that there is any such allusion there at all. The passage is about the crucifixion of Jesus and tells how 'they divided his clothes, casting lots for them'. This reads like a straightforward description of the action of the soldiers, until we turn to John 19.24 where specific reference is made to Psalm 22.18: 'They divided my clothes among them, and for my clothing they cast lots.' It is clear that in the Mark passage the reader was intended to catch this allusion as a fulfilment of scripture.

(b) Similarities with rabbinic tradition

Apart from such direct quotations and indirect allusions, however, there are other fairly obvious indications of the *rabbinic approach* to the interpretation of scripture.

There is, for example, the form of interpretation known as *peshat* found frequently in the New Testament which gives the plain sense of a passage and a straightforward application of the text. Thus the reader is exhorted to follow the good example of certain Old Testament characters whose exploits are quoted with approval and to avoid the bad example of others.

Closely associated with this is the use of quotations which reflect a close parallel between the Old Testament situation and, say, the ministry of Jesus to which they are applied. A case in point is the quotation of Isaiah 56.7 and Jeremiah 7.11 in the incident of Jesus' cleansing of the temple. The Old and New Testament scenes have a common content of indignation and confession that the Jerusalem temple was meant by God to be a place of worship for Gentiles as well as for Jews.

There are other passages, following rabbinic (and Qumran) practice, where widely separated scriptures which have some significant word or expression in common are brought together and are given what F. F. Bruce calls 'a unitive exegesis'. One of the most obvious examples of this is the evidence for an integrated messianic interpretation of various 'stone' passages in the Old Testament – the stone which the builder rejected (in Psalm 118.22), the stone in Nebuchadnezzar's dream which smashed the great image (in Daniel 2.34f.), the tested corner-stone (in Isaiah 28.16), and the rock of refuge (in Isaiah 8.14) which proves a stone of stumbling to those who refuse its refuge (a common messianic interpretation of these is given in such passages as Luke 20.17f.; Acts 4.11f.; Romans 9.33; and 1 Peter 2.6–8).

In particular we observe the occurrence in the New Testament of at least two of the recognized methods of rabbinic interpretation corresponding to the first two of the seven *middot* or rules ascribed to Hillel. (For the illustrations that follow I am indebted to C. K. Barrett, 'The Interpretation of the Old Testament in the New', in *The Cambridge History of the Bible*, Vol. 1, ed. P. R. Ackroyd and C. F. Evans, 1970, p. 385).

The first is that of inference by means of the principle *minori ad maius*, i.e. the argument from the lesser to the greater, in which the greater has usually a christological setting. Mark 2.23–28 is a case in point, where the incident recorded in I Samuel 21, in which David and his followers, against the regulations, ate holy bread from the sanctuary, is used to justify the action of Jesus and his disciples in plucking and eating ears of corn on the sabbath day. Several illustrations of a more theological character are given in the Epistle to the Hebrews and in the writings of Paul, where an Old Testament allusion is followed by the words 'how much more' with reference to the Christian dispensation. Indeed, this principle is applied not just to separate passages in the Old Testament, but in a sense to the Old Testament as a whole, which is claimed to be transcended by its fulfilment in Christ.

The second of the *middot* refers to inference by analogy, in which two passages are brought together by means of a common word or phrase. One example of this is Romans 4.2, in which Paul quotes Genesis 15.6, where it is said that Abraham's faith in God was *counted* to him as righteousness. By comparing this use of the word 'counted' with another use in Psalm 32.1 he links up the word in question with the notion of forgiveness implied in this verse, and since the verbal link joins up David (the author of Psalm 32), who is a Jew, with Abraham, who was at the time uncircumcised, therefore the blessing of forgiveness is not confined to circumcised Jews.

But whilst it is true that such subtle forms of argument are found in the New Testament, they are not at all common and not at all typical, and may in the case of the Gospels, it has been argued, be due to the evangelists rather than to Jesus himself.

Here and there in the Gospels and the letters of Paul we find certain subtleties of argument and interpretation which tend to strain merely verbal or accidental resemblances, such as the reference in Mark 12.26, where use is made of the words 'I am the God of Abraham and . . . Isaac and . . . Jacob' to prove that, since God is God of the living and not of the dead, then the patriarchs must all be still alive.

There is at least one clear case in Paul's letters of the use of allegory as a method of interpretation. This is in Galatians 4.21–31 where he allegorizes the story of Abraham's two sons, Isaac and Ishmael, and their mothers Sarah and Hagar. The two women represent covenants – the Covenant of the Promise and the Covenant of the Law. The two sons represent those born under the Law and

51

those Christians born for freedom. The thrust of the argument is that the Christians are the inheritors of the divine promise and God's true legitimate heirs. 'This,' says the apostle, 'is an allegory.'

Closely associated with this type of interpretation is the attempt to see a recapitulation, as it were, of Israel's history in the life and work of the Messiah or of the church. We think in this connection of a passage like I Corinthians 10.1–4, where Paul gives a rabbinic *midrash* on the story of Moses striking the rock in the wilderness so that water gushed forth. This 'well of water', he says, followed them wherever they went. Then in v. 4 he gives his Christian interpretation: 'The rock was Christ.' Here we have a picture of Christ, before his incarnation, delivering the Israelites and leading them through the wilderness to the promised land. The same theme is taken up in a variant reading of Jude 5 and is subsequently developed by Justin Martyr and others in the early church.

(c) Similarities with Qumran writings

More striking than these similarities with the rabbinic tradition are those between the New Testament and the Qumran writings. The actual *pesher* form of interpretation, so familiar at Qumran, is rather rare in the New Testament. An illustration of this is to be found in Romans 10.6f., in its treatment of Deuteroromy 30.12f., where the text with its meaning might be filled out like this: 'Do not say in your heart, who shall ascend into heaven? The *pesher* of this is, who shall bring Christ down? Do not say in your heart, who shall descend into the deep? The *pesher* of this is, who shall bring Christ up from the dead?'

Much more important than such similarities in *form* are the similarities in *content*. Like the Qumran Covenanters, the New Testament writers believed they were living in 'the last days' and that the key to the true understanding of scripture was to be found in the life and ministry, death and resurrection of their Lord and Master, Jesus Christ. The scriptures pointed forward to him and the salvation he was to bring. This is well illustrated in 1 Peter 1.10ff.: 'The prophets who prophesied of the grace that was to be yours searched and enquired about this salvation . . . predicting the sufferings of Christ and the subsequent glory. It was revealed to them that they were serving not themselves but you, in the things which have now been announced to you.' The mysteries recorded by the ancient prophets, says Peter in effect, have found their true interpretation and their ultimate fulfilment in Jesus. What the prophets blindly foretold, he and his fellow Christians now know as a certainty. Indeed the very word 'mystery' is used by Jesus himself in this connection as it is used in Daniel and at Qumran to indicate 'an open secret', something that has now been revealed for what it is: 'To you has been given the secret (mystery) of the Kingdom of God, but for those outside everything is in parables' (Mark 4.11f.). 'To him,' says Luke, 'all the prophets bear witness that anyone who believes in him receives forgiveness of sins through his name' (Acts 10.43).

The church's mission to the Gentile world is another mystery which has now been revealed by the Spirit (cf. Ephesians 3.4f.). The prophets of old had in fact foretold that the Gentiles would place their hope in the Davidic Messiah (cf. Romans 15), a hope which has now been fulfilled. The outpouring of the Spirit itself on the Day of Pentecost was 'that which was spoken by the prophet Joel' (Acts 2.16).

So deeply embedded is such interpretation in the New Testament tradition – in its imagery as well as in its more formal statements – that it can with some accuracy be said that the whole New Testament record itself is to be viewed as a fulfilment of the Old, and that fulfilment is focussed in the person of Jesus. He is the one to whom all the scriptures bear witness, be they Law, Prophets or Psalms. He had not come, as he himself made clear, to *destroy* the Law and the Prophets, but rather to *fulfil* them, in the sense of filling them full – giving to them their full meaning and therefore their true interpretation. The fulfilling of scripture was to be found not simply in the things that he did – as when he rode into Jerusalem on an ass's back in fulfilment of Zechariah 9.9 – and not simply in the things that he spoke – as in his summing up of the commandments in love of God and love of one's neighbour as oneself – but above all in his own person as the great deliverer, the mighty saviour, the anointed leader of whom the scriptures speak and to whose coming the faithful among God's people so eagerly look.

(d) Jesus' interpretation of scripture

The question may be asked, How did the New Testament writers learn to interpret the Old Testament scriptures in this way? The evidence we have would seem to point to none other than Jesus himself and his own spiritual awareness of his place in the unfolding purpose of God. This is seen in his frequent reference to scripture in describing his own ministry and in his quotations from such passages as Zechariah 9.14 (and his dramatization of 9.9, as noted above, when he rode in triumphant procession on 'a colt, the foal of an ass'), Isaiah 40–66 and Psalm 69. 'This,' says F. F. Bruce, 'implies something more substantial which indicates an early and well established tradition of Christian interpretation which may well go back to Jesus himself' (see op. cit, p.80). This exegesis, this 'piece of genuinely creative thinking', as C. H. Dodd calls it, is hardly likely to be the work of any of the great New Testament theologians or exegetes. The creative mind behind it is surely the mind of Jesus himself. The New Testament writers, for the most part, use scripture 'historically', as we should say, because they found in Jesus of Nazareth the climax, the fulfilment, of the age-long story of God's dealing with his people; and they were able to do so because it was to this same conclusion that Jesus himself had come: 'Today . . . in your hearing', he is reported as saying, 'this text has come true' (Luke 4.21); and again, 'Everything written in the Law of Moses and the Prophets and the Psalms must be fulfilled' (Luke 24.44). Instead of the atomizing interpretation frequently found in the rabbinic writings and elsewhere and the often super-imposed interpretation of the Qumran writings, we have what F. F. Bruce describes as 'a coherent Christian exegesis of self-contained sense-units of Old Testament Scripture' (*Biblical Exegesis in the Qumran Texts*, 1959, p.69). Starting from their own living experience of Jesus Christ, they turned to the Old Testament and found him there as its climax, its fulfilment, or as Paul would say, the 'Amen' to all God's promises, for, as he says in II Corinthians 1.20, 'all the promises of God find their Yes in him'.

IV

The Development and Meaning of Torah

I. LAW AS REVELATION

(a) A comprehensive term

The Hebrew word *torah* is usually translated by the word 'law', partly at least under the influence of the Septuagint which normally renders it by the word *nomos*. It has in fact a very wide range of meaning, from simply 'instruction' given by, say, the priest to the revelation of God made known to his people Israel and indeed to all mankind. But it has particular reference to what we know as 'the ten commandments' as recorded in Exodus 20.2–17 and comes to embrace the whole of the Pentateuch, or 'five books of Moses', which becomes for the devout Jew a supreme revelation of God's mind and will. G. F. Moore defines it as 'the comprehensive name for the divine revelation . . . in which the Jews possessed the sole standard and norm of their religion' (*Judaism* I. p.263). That divine revelation came increasingly to be associated with an authoritative written book.

(b) Covenant and law

The basis of the Hebrew law is to be found in that covenant relationship into which Israel entered with God when he delivered them out of Egypt and chose them to be his people and which finds expression in the so-called ethical decalogue of Exodus 20. Its opening words make clear that this covenant is one of divine grace: 'I am the Lord your God, who brought you out of the land of Egypt, out of the house of bondage' (20.2). He is not just a God of nature

55

who needs to be placated by fertility rites to replenish the earth. He is the God of history, known for what he is by what he does, who acts redemptively on behalf of his people.

But it is also a covenant of law – and this is not contradictory; for the law was given to make clear to the people how they might keep within the covenant, i.e. the law was itself a revelation of God's grace. Without the law it would be impossible for them to know what was or what was not a breach of the covenant relationship. The motive for keeping the law was not that the people might win God's favour and so by their achievement be accepted by God (cf. Deuteronomy 9.5f.). It was simply that the people might be shown what was meant by obedience to the will of God and so remain within the covenant. The law itself was a revelation of God's love and grace (cf. Deuteronomy 7.8f.).

(c) Moses: priest and lawgiver

The unique place of Moses as 'lawgiver supreme' has an established place in Hebrew tradition. In Exodus 18 we read of Moses sitting as judge of the people, giving decisions on all kinds of matters appertaining to the people of Israel and, when the task becomes too onerous, sharing it with seventy elders.

It is of some significance that Moses, as legislator, in so doing acts in a priestly capacity (cf. Psalm 99.6), for this work of giving 'decisions' (*toroth*) was continued and elaborated in the years to come by the priestly body in Israel. Acting in the name of their leader and progenitor Moses, with each succeeding generation acting on the precedent of those who had gone before, the priests built up a definite hereditary law based on custom and tradition which gave them an advantage over the 'elders' or ordinary lay judges of the people's court.

It is against this background that we are to understand the ascription of such writings as Deuteronomy and much exilic or post-exilic legislation to Moses, who is regarded as the author of all law-giving. Just as the Psalms are credited to David, the father of psalmody, and such wisdom books as Proverbs (in part), Ecclesiastes and the Book of Wisdom are credited to Solomon as the fountain-head of all wisdom, so the law in all its diverse manifestations can be traced back to Moses who stands at its very beginnings and is the inspiration of all that follows. Just as an elder son's portion of Elijah's spirit could rest upon Elisha, and Moses' spirit could be imparted to the seventy elders for their task of judging the people, so the priest could take his place in a long line of priestly tradition and declare concerning his own pronouncements, 'Thus spake Yahweh unto Moses' just as honestly and just as powerfully as the prophet could say 'Thus saith the Lord'.

(d) A written code

In course of time this accumulation of *toroth*, which would be for the most part oral, was put into writing in a number of 'codes' or collections. The process was no doubt a gradual one, stretching back over several generations. The period of the exile was important in this respect, when the priests in particular set down in writing the customs and usages of the temple which had been destroyed, and began to develop codes of laws adapted to the needs of the restored community as they would wish to see it. This process of recording and supplementing earlier teaching reached its culmination during or just following the time of Ezra, whose Law Book, which he brought back from Babylon, is probably to be identified either with the Pentateuch or with the Priestly Code which was soon to be used as the framework of the Pentateuch.

The significant factor for our purpose is that from the time of Ezra onwards it was believed that the divine revelation, derived from Moses and formulated under the inspiration of the Holy Spirit, found its supreme expression in the written code of law contained in the Pentateuch, so that the word 'Torah' comes at last to be used with special reference to the five 'books of Moses'. The importance of this development can be seen from the place given to the written Torah by the Chronicler, writing perhaps around the year 350 BC. We observe that there is a 'much stronger emphasis on Moses and the Torah in Chronicles than in the corresponding books of the Deuteronomist. The name of Moses occurs only twelve times in Samuel and Kings, but thirty-one times in the works of the Chronicler. The term Torah is found only twelve times in the former, and about forty times in the latter.' It is presented as 'a fixed, authoritative body of material' treating of Pentateuchal legislation of various kinds and is set up as 'the official standard according to which the life and activity of nation and individuals were judged' (Jacob M. Myers, *Chronicles*, Anchor Bible, 1965, pp. lxviiif.). In course of time the authoritative character of the Pentateuchal writings became more clearly defined, so that, as we have seen, even before the beginning of the Hellenistic period their 'canonical' status had come to be recognized.

(e) Symbol of Judaism

From this time on the emphasis falls more and more on the need for the people to fulfil the letter of the Law, so that the observance of the Law acquires a central significance in a man's relationship with God. As a result, the scribe now comes forward to take over many of the duties which hitherto had been regarded as the prerogative of the priest; the preservation and study of the Law now becomes of primary importance. The sacrificial worship of the temple continued to occupy an important place in the life and devotions of the people; but just as the learning of the scribe was seen to be more important than the cultic activity of the priest, so the observance of the Law was seen to be more central than the observance of the temple ritual. Or perhaps we can more safely put it this way: the temple ritual, to be correct and acceptable to God, had to be carried out in conformity with the Law, so that the Law was recognized as the regulating principle by which the cult was ordered and which gave sense to the temple service as a whole. The temple continued to be revered; but increasingly the people's faith found its focus rather in the Torah, which came to be recognized by friend and foe alike as *the* symbol of Judaism. Long before the outbreak of the Maccabaean Revolt, then, the Jews had become 'the people of the Book', as can be illustrated by such writings as the Book of Tobit (before 200 BC), which lays great stress on the keeping of the Law; the Wisdom of Ben Sira (about 180 BC) which, as we shall see, likens Torah to Wisdom and refers to it as the supreme gift of God; and the Book of Jubilees (second century BC) which claims that the Torah is not only perfect but is also eternal.

It was natural that the Jews of the Dispersion, for example, should turn for consolation to the Holy Book, deprived as they were of the Holy Temple; the spread of the synagogues and the schools in both the Dispersion and Palestine would also enhance its reputation and engender in the hearts of many pious Jews an enthusiastic and even fanatical devotion to the Torah. Thus when the priest Mattathias at Modein summoned the people to resist the orders of Antiochus Epiphanes and to fight in defence of their religion, it was to the Torah that he pointed as the rallying point of revolt: 'Whosoever is jealous for the Torah, and maintains the covenant, let him come after me' (1 Maccabees 2.27). The Torah, in the form of the sacred scrolls of the Law, was the outward symbol of that inner faith which they had received from their fathers and which they must never betray. Antiochus Epiphanes readily recognized this fact, for in the persecution which followed we are told that his soldiers 'rent in pieces the books of the Law which they found and set them on fire. And wheresoever was found with any a book of the covenant, and if any consented to the law, the King's sentence delivered him unto death' (1 Maccabees 1.56–57). An assault on the Torah was an assault on the whole Jewish faith.

(f) Law as oral tradition

A religion which is based on a book whose writings and laws regulate and determine its life inevitably finds areas of life for which these regulations have no clear and direct guidance to give. The result is either an adaptation of the text to fit the circumstance or the development of an oral tradition alongside the text which acquires an authority of its own. We have seen in the previous chapter that both these lines were followed by the interpreters of early Judaism. In the case of oral tradition, laws came to be formed relating to prevailing custom among the people, but which could not be justified simply by reference to the written Torah. Nevertheless they acquired authority on at least two grounds: they formed a 'fence round the Torah' (Pirke' Abot 1.1), giving warning in advance of a possible breach of the Law (e.g. forbidding even the handling and not just the use of tools on the sabbath), and they carried the weight not only of revered teachers but also of a long line of tradition which, it was believed, went right back to Moses himself. Inspired by the Spirit of God, he was the source of written law and oral tradition alike. Together they formed but one entity, a divine revelation by which Israel could remain the covenant people of God.

2. LAW AS LEGISLATION

(a) A shift of emphasis

We have seen that essentially Torah was to be understood in terms of revelation and, in particular, as a gift of God's grace to his people, enabling them to remain within the covenant made with their fathers. Thus, from early times, covenant and Torah were closely related to each other. This relationship came to be spelt out more rigidly in the post-exilic period and in the two centuries or so before the Christian era; so that the Torah is regarded as 'the book of the covenant'.

During this time we can detect a change of emphasis in the popular imagination from 'faithfulness within the covenant' to 'obedience to the Torah'. Obedience to the Law of God was all-important as the indispensable condition of their acceptance as heirs of the covenant; disobedience meant rejection of the covenant and the God-given promises that went with it. It is too much to say with John Bright that 'here law has ceased to be the definition of the requisite response to the gracious acts of God and becomes the means by which men might achieve the divine favour and become worthy of the promises' (*The History of Israel*, 1962, p.428). Nevertheless, covenant and Torah were inseparably related: to keep the Law was to keep the covenant and to break the Law was to break the covenant. In such circumstances it was all-important, therefore, that the Law should be defined, applied and obeyed.

(b) Outward observances

An indication of this trend can be seen in the stress which is now laid on outward observances as marks of the religious life. Circumcision, for example, which had been given prominence as a distinctive characteristic of the Jewish faith in immediate post-exilic days, now became of much greater importance as the Hellenistic period advanced; to submit oneself to 'uncircumcision' was to 'forsake the Holy Covenant' (I Maccabees 1.15). Similarly, sabbath observance was regarded as of such vital importance that men chose to be slaughtered rather than fight on that sacred day (cf. I Maccabees 2.29–38; II Maccabees 6.11). Ritual cleanness and obedience to the letter of the Law were believed to be of primary importance. Hence the Jews' fanatical refusal to eat swine's flesh, their strict observance of dietary laws, fasting, tithing and all ceremonial requirements; hence, too, their bitter hatred of idolatry of every kind, even if it were only the statue of an eagle over the gate of the temple (cf. *Antiquities* XVII.vi.2).

(c) A means of merit

Judaism had no inhibitions about drawing the logical conclusion from all this, which was that obedience to the Law would bring reward and disobedience would bring punishment. Not only was this conclusion logical, it was also scriptural and had been expounded by inspired priests and prophets from at least the time of Deuteronomy onwards. The danger was that such obedience to the Law might come to be regarded as a means of gaining God's favour rather than as a ready response to the gracious acts of God in saving his people. Quoting a certain Rabbi Hananiah ben Akashya, G. F. Moore concludes: 'The multiplied commandments (to which the Rabbi refers) are to give Israel ampler opportunity to acquire merit by obedience and by avoiding transgression' (*Judaism* II, pp. 92f.). Such merit, according to II Esdras and II Baruch (apocalypses of the late first century AD), is stored up in heaven; the books will one day be opened and the treasuries of the righteous as well as the sins of the wicked will be made plain (cf. II Esdras 7.77; II Baruch 24.1). Or again, in Tobit 4.8ff. (before 200 BC) we read, 'Do not be afraid to give alms . . ., for thou layest up a good treasure for thyself against the day of necessity: because alms delivereth from death, and suffereth not to come into darkness.' To give alms was in fact to go beyond the strict letter of the law and so particular merit attached to it. It is of interest to observe that as early as Ben Sira (c. 180 BC) the Greek word *eleĕmosunēn*, which is used seventeen

61

times in the Septuagint to translate the Hebrew word *ṣedaqah* meaning 'righteousness', is used with the meaning 'almsgiving'.

It would be wrong, however, to imagine that Judaism was unaware of the dangers involved in such an attitude towards the Law or in any merely formal obedience to its commandments. The need for repentance remained central, as did the intention of the one involved. So important indeed is repentance that it is regarded as existing even before creation itself. What was needed was not just a formal response to a code of law, but a repentant response to a God of grace. This was still the ideal, and there were many in Judaism who pursued it.

(d) Piety and devotion

There were many who recognized and responded to the Law's high ethical demand and for whom its observance was a delight (cf. Psalm 19.7–14). The literature of this period gives ample proof of the growth of true piety, deep devotion and a reverence for righteousness (cf. Ben Sira 1.11ff.). The 'meek' and 'humble', of whom we read in the Psalms and elsewhere, belong as truly to Judaism as the legalists and literalists of their day. But all of them together swore allegiance to the Law whether they belonged to the Pharisaic party or not. The various parties in Judaism disagreed (often profoundly) over the precise interpretation of the Law, but behind this disagreement there lay a deep loyalty on the part of all to the Law itself. The Pharisees prided themselves in being 'the Torah party'; but all the other parties could with equal enthusiasm claim the same title for themselves, not least the Essenes who, as Josephus tells us, spent much time in the study of the Torah and other sacred books of which they took the greatest possible care. This is confirmed by the Dead Sea Scrolls, which tell us that whenever the members of the Qumran council met together in groups of ten, as was the custom, some member of the group was always engaged in study or exposition. Ordinary members of the community were to devote the first third of every night to reading 'the book', studying the Law and responding with the appropriate blessings. Such a passage as Ben Sira 39.1–11 demonstrates quite clearly that the ideal Jew, where Jewish piety was concerned, was not the priest devoted to the sacrifices of the temple, but rather the layman dedicated to the reading and study of the Law. A man's standing before God was determined not so much by the nation or race to which he belonged as by his attitude to the Law. This, as we shall see presently, brought even the Gentile within the scope of God's salvation, in theory at least, for he, like the Jew, would be judged by his response to or rejection of the Law.

(e) Jesus and the Pharisees

The attitude of Jesus to the Law and in particular to the Pharisees as expounders of the Law has long been a point of debate among scholars. It has been argued, for example, that it was his opposition to the legalism of Judaism, breeding self-righteousness on the part of its adherents, that led to his clash with the authorities and ended in his death. According to the Gospel record with its recurring phrase 'woe to you, scribes and Pharisees, hypocrites' and the illustrations given there of formalism, religiosity and self-righteousness, the charge of legalism would appear to be fully justified (cf. Matthew 6.1–8, 16–18; 23.5–7, 23–26; Luke 15.2, 25–32; 16.14f.; 18.9–14).

Some scholars argue that contemporary Jewish literature and the Gospels themselves give ample evidence that 'Pharisaism and Judaism were not as such legalistic' (E. P. Sanders, *Jesus and Judaism*, 1985, p.279). In substantiating this claim Sanders has to argue that much of the 'evidence' does not reflect the mind of Jesus himself, but rather the theological thinking of the early church. He concedes that criticism of religious hypocrisy and self-righteousness is still to be found there, but argues strongly that, even if this is so, it does not give the reason for Jesus' conflict with Judaism. Indeed, in a number of respects Jesus himself was more strict in his adherence to the Law and in his application of it than the Pharisees whom he condemned.

It has been pointed out in support of this contention, that the early disciples give no indication that Jesus had opposed the Law and that even Paul makes no reference to such a thing where we might have expected it – in his argument in the Epistle to the

Romans that the basis of salvation is to be found in faith in Christ and not in keeping the Torah.

Others disagree with such findings and remain unconvinced by what they would regard as arbitrary treatment of the text and by argument from silence and see in Jesus one who criticized not just the self-righteous application of the Law, but the Law itself as the supreme revelation of the divine will.

3. LAW AND ITS ATTRIBUTES

An examination of the Jewish understanding of law at the beginning of the Christian era runs into two difficulties. One is, as has already been indicated, the different meanings given to *torah* itself, ranging from the divine revelation made known to Israel (or to all mankind) right down to the minutiae of rules and regulations relating to the ordering of every aspect of life. The other is the precise dating of the rabbinic material on which so much of our information depends. Most of this, in its written form, is later than the first century AD, but much of what is 'codified' there (e.g. in the Mishnah) no doubt reflects an earlier pre-Christian situation.

Of particular interest is the close association, at this time and earlier, between Law and Wisdom and the serious attempt made to bring into synthesis law and reason. In Baruch 4.1, for example, (dating from the first century AD or earlier) Wisdom is described as 'the book of the commandments of God and the Law that endures for ever'; and in Ben Sira 24.23 (c. 180 BC) the Law is the very foundation of Wisdom and is referred to as the supreme gift of God. Such references remind us that, throughout the whole of this period, there was a very close relationship between the practice of the Law and the pursuit of Wisdom. The teachers of Wisdom, for example, who were an active religious force at this time, were also teachers of the Law. The good life, which was the goal of true Wisdom, was to be found in obedience to the Law, a theme which of course can be traced back to the Book of Proverbs and some of the later Psalms (e.g. 1; 49; 112; 119) and is prominent in the later apocryphal and rabbinic literature.

Once Wisdom had in this way come to be associated with

the Law, it was not long before the attributes and even the personification of Wisdom came to be attributed to it also.

(a) Pre-existent and eternal

According to Jewish tradition there were seven things created before the creation of the world. The first of these is the Law (with a clear reference to the function of Wisdom as indicated in Proverbs 8.22). In the beginning when God set about the creation of the world, he first took counsel with Torah which he appointed overseer for every act of creation and mediator between himself and his creation. By way of illustration G. F. Moore quotes this passage from Genesis Rabbah: 'As a rule an earthly King who is building a palace does not build it according to his own ideas, but to those of an architect; and the architect does not build it out of his own head, but has parchments or tablets to know how he should make the rooms and openings; so God looked into the Law and created the world' (*Judaism* I, p.267).

A presupposition of this mediatorial function of the Torah is that it was pre-existent and indeed eternal. A famous dictum in the Mishnah tract Pirke' Abot states that, in effect, it was of the very substance of life itself, for 'the stability of the world rests on three things: on the law, on worship and on deeds of personal kindness' (1.2). So also in the Book of Jubilees, dating from the second century BC, where it is stated that many of its enactments and institutions originated in very early times and indeed came into being before creation itself. A certain Rabbi Benaiah at a later date goes a stage further and lays down that the whole universe, including Israel and all mankind, was brought into being in the first place for the sake of the Torah.

(b) Immutable

This association of the Law with Wisdom, however, emphasizes not only its mediatorial function and pre-existent and eternal state, but also its immutability. In the words of W. D. Davies: 'The Torah . . . had been given to Moses by Yahweh. As the gift of Yahweh and as the ground plan of the universe it could not but be perfect and unchangeable; it was impossible that it should ever be

65

forgotten; no prophet could arise who would change it and no new Moses should ever appear to introduce another law to replace it' (*Torah in the Messianic Age*, 1952, pp. 51f.). G. F. Moore quotes in this connection a passage from Philo in which he contrasts the ever changing laws of the nations with the unchanging Torah of Israel: 'The provisions of this law alone, stable, unmoved, unshaken, as it were stamped with the seal of nature itself, remain in fixity from the day they were written until now, and for the future we expect them to abide to all time as immortal, so long as the sun and moon and the whole heaven and the world exist' (*Judaism* I, p.269). This same rabbinic viewpoint is strongly represented in the sayings of Jesus in the Gospels, as in Matthew 5.18f., for example: 'For truly I say to you till heaven and earth pass away, not an iota, not a dot, will pass from the law until all is accomplished. Whoever then relaxes one of the least of these commandments and teaches men so, shall be called least in the Kingdom of heaven.' So also in Luke 16.17: 'It is easier for heaven and earth to pass away, than for one dot of the law to become void'.

(c) Universal

Along with this notion of the immutability of the Law went also the idea of its universality. It existed, like Wisdom, with a validity of its own. As we have seen, the Jews could not consider that there had been a time when the Law had not been in existence and exercised its authority. This had at least two implications in terms of its universality.

For one thing it was unthinkable that the Patriarchs before Moses should have been without the Law, and so in the Book of Jubilees, for example, it is stated that the whole system of religious festivals and the detailed ritual of sacrifice had been introduced by Noah, Abraham, Isaac and Jacob even although it is stated that such things were made known to Moses on Mount Sinai. Indeed, in one rabbinic source it is categorically stated that 'Abraham our father kept the whole Torah before it had been given' (Kiddushin 4.14).

Secondly, the conviction grew that all men, be they Jews or Gentiles, were under obligation to keep the Law. Six commandments, it was believed, had been given to Adam, applicable to all mankind. These commandments, together with a seventh, were given after the Flood to Noah for his (Gentile) descendants; but all to no avail. But such speculation went further still: even the Law revealed by God to Moses on Sinai had itself been fully revealed to the Gentiles. But Israel, alone of all the nations, had accepted the offer of it and responded to it. All the other nations had rejected it out of hand and so are without the Law. Indeed it is stated that the Law was given in the wilderness and not in Israel lest the Gentiles should complain of preferential treatment having been given to the Jews. According to Jewish tradition based on Genesis 10, the nations of the world numbered seventy; hence the belief that the Law at Sinai was proclaimed by God or interpreted by Moses in seventy languages; the nations sent their scribes who copied it in seventy different tongues and this, we recall, was the number (in one tradition at least) of those engaged in the translation of the Pentateuch into Greek. God knew that the nations would so reject the Law; but he gave them no ground for excuse. Israel alone received it with joy and bound itself to live according to its rules. A concession is made by some authorities, however, in the case of individual Gentiles, as distinct from nations, who are held in high esteem because they occupy themselves with the study of the Torah.

4. LAW AND ITS DEMANDS

(a) A sense of despair

The conviction grew, and became most evident in the first century of the Christian era, that so strict were the demands of the Law that, on any interpretation of it, it was utterly impossible for any man, Gentile or Jew, to keep it.

This attitude is made specially clear in II Esdras, written towards the end of the first Christian century by a Jew who himself belonged to the circle of Law teachers. He regards the Law as a divine gift to Israel, but he has to confess that it is utterly inadequate to meet man's deepest needs and to solve the great moral problems with which life confronts him. Man trembles before the Law; he needs mercy, not the award of the Law, for all have sinned (8.35). Powerful though the Law is, it has been prevented from bearing fruit by reason of the opposition of sin. Israel has received the commandments, but its people have not kept them; they have obtained the Law, but have dealt unfaithfully with what they received (7.72). The Law leads only to condemnation and death, for 'we who have received the Law and sinned will perish' (9.36). To the human race, doomed to sin, the promises of the Law are a mockery (7.116–131). The most that the writer can hope for is that a few will be saved (9.15), either through good works (7.77) or through the divine compassion (7.139). It is hardly necessary to draw attention to the close parallel here with the thought of the apostle Paul who, in Romans 3.20 for example, states that 'through the law comes knowledge of sin'. This sense of impotence and despair must have been widespread at this time within Judaism and, as we know, led to attempts to solve what to the pious Jew was a profound religious and moral problem.

(b) In the messianic age

Such assurances as were given did little to remove the sense of despondency felt by so many that the Law could not of itself bring salvation because all had sinned. All that could be hoped for was the belief, prevalent in the first Christian century, that, just as the age of chaos which had lasted for two thousand years had given way to the age of the Torah which would similarly last two thousand years, so the age of Torah itself would give way to the age of the Messiah.

This cannot mean that, with the coming of the Messiah, the Law of God will be of none effect, for even God himself, it is said, will be engaged in the study of it in the age to come! Rather, it will be a time when difficulties in the Law will at last be explained and understood. In later rabbinic writings references are made to the Messiah bringing with him a *new Torah*. W. D. Davies and others have argued that, although these references are few and late, they nevertheless reflect earlier beliefs. Indeed the absence of earlier references, in say the first Christian century, may be due to a reaction against Christian teaching on this point. Be that as it may, any new Torah envisaged in the messianic age would be new, not in the sense of nullifying, but rather in the sense of fulfilling the old.

(c) The law of Christ

We have seen that the New Testament affirms the Law given by God to his people Israel (cf. Matthew 5.18f.; Luke 16.17), but it also sees its fulfilment in Jesus Christ their Lord. The assured belief is expressed, moreover, that the new Torah is to be inaugurated in the messianic age whose coming is to be identified with the incarnation of Jesus and realized in power in his death and resurrection. The coming of Jesus meant for the Christians that they were, in a new sense, from that time on living in the messianic age and that their lives had been brought under a new rule of law. The Gospel of Matthew, as we have noted, indicates that the words of Jesus were a fulfilment of the Law and the Prophets and themselves constituted the Torah of the Messiah of populur expectation. In somewhat the same way the apostle Paul can bid his readers, 'Bear one another's burdens and so fulfil the law of Christ' (Galatians 6.2), whilst in John's Gospel reference is made to the need to keep 'the commandments' of Christ (14.15) which are elsewhere described as 'a new commandment' (13.34; cf. I John 2.7ff.).

This 'new commandment' or 'new law' is the accompaniment of 'a new covenant' which, as it were, sweeps up and replaces the detailed legal regulations which in the present form of the tradition accompany the Sinai covenant. It is in fact the law of love. The just requirement of the Law, says Jesus, is nothing less than love to God and love to one's neighbour (cf. Luke 10.25–28), or, as Paul puts it in Romans 13.10, 'The fulfilling of the law is love', the sum total of all the commandments. The new covenant and the new law by which we keep within the covenant agree with each other, for both declare that God is love.

But this demonstration of the 'new law' is to be seen not just in the words of Jesus; it is to be seen supremely in his very life and person who is described as 'the way, the truth and the life'. In him we have what W. D. Davies calls 'a personification of Torah in Christ' which goes beyond anything to be found in the Jewish sources (op. cit., p.93). Any expectations the Jews may have had of a new Torah matching the glories of the age to come were not only fulfilled but far transcended in him.

V

Prayer and Mediation

From very early times the Hebrews were deeply conscious of the holiness and 'otherness' of God upon whose face no man could look and live. This sense of the divine transcendence is particularly noticeable in the exilic and post-exilic literature and finds ample illustration in the literature of the intertestamental period. One indication of this is to be seen in the reluctance to use the divine name 'Yahweh' and to substitute for it such high-sounding titles as 'Most High God', 'Ancient of Days', 'Lord of Spirits' and so on.

At the same time it was believed that this 'transcendent' God (the word is not altogether apt with its un-Hebraic philosophical overtones) was nevertheless close at hand and could be approached in prayer and supplication, reverently but confidently. The 'God afar off' was also 'the God near at hand'; the 'holy God' was 'the one who forgives and saves'; the 'creator of the ends of the earth' was 'the one who hears the cry of the oppressed'. The same emphases are reflected in the New Testament when, for example, Jesus addresses God as 'holy Father' (cf. John 17.11) or when he teaches his disciples to pray, saying, 'Our Father, who art in heaven, hallowed be Thy name' (cf. Matthew 6.9; Luke 11.2). The holy God is the approachable God who can be sought and found through prayer.

Generally speaking, access to God through prayer is immediate and direct, without the need for any mediation on the part of another. Sometimes, however, such prayers require the good offices of an angelic mediator to carry the prayer into God's presence, as

71

it were, or to bring back God's reply either in word or in deed. Not infrequently these angel intermediaries appear in the form of 'a man' or 'a young man', as in the resurrection story in the Gospels (cf. Luke 24.4). Illustrations of this are, of course, to be found even in the earlier parts of the Old Testament (e.g. Genesis 18.1ff.; 19.1ff.), but it is in the later biblical and post-biblical literature that mediation of this kind comes into much greater prominence, a phenomenon which no doubt owes not a little to the influence of that dualism and syncretism in religion which became widespread during the Hellenistic period.

Intermediaries of a different kind also appear in the literature of this period which are difficult to define. They represent personifications or expressions of divine qualities rather than 'creatures' in their own right, sharing and demonstrating some of the properties and characteristics of God himself. Prominent among these are Wisdom, Spirit and Logos which have an important role to play in the New Testament and in Christian theology generally.

I. PRAYER AND RESPONSE

(a) Prayer and piety

We have already seen that the life of many Jews in the post-exilic and intertestamental periods was marked by a deep piety and spirituality, expressing itself in public and private prayer and in the study of the sacred scriptures. Illustrations of this are to be found in the New Testament in the persons of Simeon who, it is said, was 'righteous and devout, looking for the consolation of Israel' (Luke 2.25), and of Anna who 'did not depart from the temple, worshipping with fasting and prayer night and day' (Luke 2.37).

Such devotion was fostered by two things in particular. The first was the temple and its services of worship in which the psalms were read and sung. Some of these probably had their origin in private devotion and were later adapted for public, liturgical use. Whatever their origin and date of composition they were at this time an aid to prayer and a witness to that spirituality which marked the temple worship as a whole. The second was the synagogue worship with its emphasis on prayer and the study of the Law. These spiritual exercises did not replace the temple worship; rather, they supplemented it, so that in course of time the prayers of the synagogue came to be regarded by many as the spiritual equivalent of the sacrifices of the temple. In this way they prepared for the time when the sacrifices of the temple would be no longer possible.

The close relationship between temple and synagogue is well illustrated not only by the use of the psalms in each, but also by the lay delegations who accompanied their priests twice each year to Jerusalem from the twenty-four districts into which the country was divided (cf. I Chronicles 23–25); whilst they ministered in the temple, the rest of the people in their home town or village read the scriptures and offered prayers. We are reminded too of Daniel who, facing Jerusalem and the temple there, prayed three times daily, corresponding to the morning and evening sacrifices and the burning of the scraps at sunset (cf. Daniel 6.11 and also Judith 9.1). Such incidents show a clear picture of the prevailing piety of early Judaism both in formal worship and in private devotion.

Two sources are of particular interest in demonstrating the content of formal or liturgical prayer and the depth and scope of private prayer at this time. Both, in their present written form, are later than the first century AD, but undoubtedly reflect pre-Christian usage. The first is the so-called *Shemoneh Esreh* or Eighteen Benedictions used in synagogue worship, which breathes the spirit of Old Testament piety and expresses the deep devotion of the psalms. The second is the first tractate in the Mishnah called *Berakot* or Blessings. Prayers and blessings are prescribed there for almost every aspect of daily life – for craftsmen on the top of a tree or the roof of a building, for a bridegroom on his first night, for a mourner, for slaves, for those on a ship or a raft, for grace before meals; there are prayers for those who witness violent storms of thunder and lightning, who build a house, who enter or leave a town and so on. The fact that such prayers were *prescribed* for use could lead to formalism in religion; but behind this 'codifying' we can sense the deep devotion of men and women who sought and found immediate and intimate fellowship with God.

This fact is well illustrated in the books of the Apocrypha, and indeed of the Pseudepigrapha, where, almost without exception, reference is made to prayer being offered in all kinds of situations and with all kinds of request. These vary from cries for help in time of war (e.g. Judith 6.19,21; I Maccabees 4.32; II Maccabees 1.8) to prayers for protection on a journey (e.g. Tobit 4.19; Jubilees 12.21), from thanksgiving for food and drink (e.g. Aristeas 184, 185; Sibylline Oracles IV, 24–26) to prayers for the birth of a child (e.g. Testament of Judah 19.2), from petitions for health and healing (e.g. Tobit 8.17; Ben Sira 38.9) to intercessions for the nation (e.g. Ben Sira 36.10, 11; Psalms of Solomon 17.23ff.), from confession of sin (e.g. II Maccabees 12.41ff.; Ben Sira 21.1) to expressions of spontaneous praise (e.g. Psalms of Solomon 3.1).

(b) The divine response

It can be seen, then, that access to God in prayer was open to all who called upon him, irrespective of circumstances or position in society: 'The prayer of a poor man,' says Ben Sira, 'goes from his lips to the ears of God' (21.5) who speedily responds to his prayer. Sometimes that response is made directly by God, without any visible or audible manifestation – the prayer is granted and help is given. At other times it comes in the form of a dream or a vision. This is a fairly common occurrence in the writings of the intertestamental period, from the Book of Daniel onwards. They are not simply subjective experiences arising out of a person's subconscious, as we should say; they are sent forth by God as media and vehicles of revelation (cf. 1 Enoch 13.4; II Baruch 55.3). Closely associated with these are recorded occurrences of apparitions which appear suddenly in the sky and through which God makes his purpose known. A case in point is the 'magnificently caperisoned horse with a rider of frightening mien' which terrified Seleucus's chief minister Heliodorus, and two young men, 'gloriously beautiful and splendidly dressed' who 'scourged him continuously' (II Maccabees 3.23–28), or the 'five resplendent men on horses with golden bridles' that appeared from heaven in defence of Judas (II Maccabees 10.29f.).

At other times again, the response comes in the shape of a voice giving encouragement (e.g. II Enoch 22.4f.) or instruction (e.g. I

Enoch 81.1) or warning (e.g. Apocalypse of Moses 23.1ff.) or explanation (e.g. II Baruch 4.1). We recognize here the *bath qol* of rabbinic tradition in which is heard the echo of God's voice which corresponds in the sphere of hearing to the dream or vision in the sphere of seeing.

In the New Testament we recall the experience of the dream or the vision in response to prayer, as in the case of Cornelius who was bidden to make contact with Peter (cf. Acts 10.1ff.), or of Paul who was bidden to go to the Gentiles (cf. Acts 22.17ff.); or of the voice from heaven at Jesus' baptism (cf. Luke 3.22) and transfiguration (cf. Luke 9.35) or at Saul's conversion on the Damascus road (cf. Acts 9.7; 22.9). Here, too, we find a God who hears and answers prayer, whose ear is ever open to their cry. There is freedom of access and readiness of response.

2. ANGELS AS INTERMEDIARIES

But although there is this deep sense of free and full entry into the presence of God through prayer, the awareness grew during the intertestamental period of the important role played by angels not only in enabling such prayers to reach the ear of God but also, and more so, in being the instruments in God's hands of carrying out his holy purposes in the world. In the Book of Tobit, for example, where prayer is at its most immediate and intimate, the archangel Raphael is introduced as one of those who 'present the prayers of the saints and enter into the presence of the Holy One' (12.15). But more than that, it is this same Raphael who, in the appearance of a man, is said to accompany Tobias on a journey he is about to make. The words used to describe the incident are as 'immediate and intimate' as the prayers themselves: 'Then Tobit said to (Tobias), "Find a man who will go with you and I will pay him wages. . ." So he went to look for a man, and he found Raphael, who was an angel, but Tobias did not know it. . . And his father said to him, "Go with this man; God who dwells in heaven will prosper your way, and may his angel attend you." So they both went out and departed, and the young man's dog was with them' (Tobit 5.3–5, 16). It was as natural for a man to be accompanied by an angel as it was for him to be accompanied by his dog! We are reminded here of the *fravashis* of Persian belief which are described as 'powerful, pre-eminent guardian angels' whose swiftness, might, beauty, helpfulness and friendship are shown to all true believers (Yasht 13.1). Such guardian angels are, of course, alluded to also in the New Testament scriptures, in the Gospels (cf. Matthew 18.10).

(a) In the Old Testament

Belief in angels, of course, was no new phenomenon in Hebrew thought, for in the Old Testament frequent reference is made, at different points in its development, to the presence alongside Yahweh of supernatural beings of various kinds. When we use the expression 'ethical monotheism' with reference to the prophetic teaching of the Old Testament, we have to understand that the word 'monotheism' did not mean for the Hebrews what it means for us today. It did not signify a belief in the existence of one celestial being living over against men and the created world in isolated majesty. On the contrary, the spiritual world, where God is, is filled with such creatures as cherubim, seraphim, 'heavenly beings' and 'messengers' of all kinds who share the nature, though not the being, of God himself. Indeed, in a number of places, they are actually referred to as 'gods' (cf. Pss.86.8; 96.4; 135.5) and elsewhere are represented as members of God's heavenly council or parliament, among whom he divides the nations of the earth so that they rule over them. An interesting passage in this connection is Deuteronomy 32.8 which, according to the Hebrew text, states that the nations of the earth were divided up 'according to the number of the children of Israel' (which is elsewhere given as seventy, cf. Exodus 1.5). The reading of the Septuagint (supported by a Hebrew text from Qumran) states that God divided up the Gentile nations 'according to the number of the angels of God'. On this reckoning, the remarkable growth of angelology at this time may have resulted from a demoting, as it were, of the gods of the heathen brought about by the increasing awareness of the transcendence of the God of Israel.

(b) A hierarchical system

It was during the Hellenistic period especially that this belief in angels and spirit-beings generally underwent the greatest development so that as early as the time of Daniel there had emerged a prolific angelic tradition in which, it is said, 'a thousand thousands' ministered to the Ancient of Days, and 'ten thousand times ten thousand stood before him' (7.10; cf. Revelation 5.11).

Even more significant is the fact that these angels are now arranged in a hierarchical system or like a well-drilled army with its officers and 'other ranks'. In the Book of Jubilees, for example, we have three distinct ranks specified: first, 'the angels of the presence'; second, 'the angels of sanctification'; and third, the angels set over the phenomena of nature. The first two, called 'these two great classes', are to be distinguished from the third 'inferior' class (cf. Jubilees 2.18).

Those who belong to the 'officer-class' are given specific duties to perform. It is they, for example, who 'minister before the Lord continually' (Jubilees 30.18), and 'guard God's throne' (I Enoch 71.7); they intercede on behalf of men (I Enoch 15.2) and act as mediators between men and God (cf. I Enoch 99.3) as in the case of Raphael in the Book of Tobit; it is this same Raphael who acts as mediator between God and men when he is sent to bring healing to Tobit and his niece Sarah (3.16f.); besides all this, they make known to men the secrets of God's hidden purpose and guide men in the right path.

(c) Titles and names

But these high-ranking angels are to be identified not only by the functions they perform, but also by the titles they hold and by the fact that now for the first time in Hebrew literature they are given personal names. The 'commanders-in-chief' are identified as seven, or in another tradition four, archangels. Their names are Uriel, Raphael, Raguel, Michael, Saraqael, Gabriel and Remiel, each with his own function and responsibilities in carrying out the will of God. The custom of naming angels is to be found in Persian sources, and the number seven with reference to the archangels may reflect the Babylonian worship of the seven 'planets', or more accurately the five planets together with the sun and the moon.

This development is of importance for our understanding of the notion of divine mediation. Strictly speaking, God can be mediated only by someone or something virtually identifiable with him – as, for example, the angel of the presence in the Old Testament. As soon as an angel becomes known by his own name and acquires a character and personality quite distinct from that of the Godhead, he becomes a representative of God rather than a mediator in the truest sense of that word.

This representative, rather than mediatorial, function of the angels is implied in Galatians 3.19, for example, which refers to the tradition, preserved in the Septuagint of Deuteronomy 33.2 (cf. Hebrews 2.2; Acts 7.38, 53), that the Law at Sinai was given not directly by God, but through his angelic representatives and so lacked the authority of God's own life-giving word. By way of contrast, Jesus can be described in 1 Timothy 2.5 as the 'one mediator between God and man'; this is the prevailing theme of such a writing as the Epistle to the Hebrews where Jesus is presented as mediator of the New Covenant by virtue of the fact that he is 'the effulgence of his glory and the very image of his substance'; he has become 'so much better than the angels, having inherited a more excellent name than they' (1.3, 4).

(d) Guardians of the nations

Reference has already been made to the Septuagint reading of Deuteronomy 32.8, where the angels are set as guardians or rulers of the nations. This idea is greatly developed during the intertestamental period, beginning with the Book of Daniel which tells how the guardian angel of Israel enters into battle with those of Persia and Greece and so effects victory for God's own people over their enemies. These guardian angels, it would appear, form a heavenly counterpart of the Gentile rulers into whose power God had, from time to time, delivered his people by reason of their sins. Wars on earth likewise had their counterpart in wars in heaven between the several guardian angels and their hosts. Indeed, according to some writers, the war in heaven determined the corresponding war on earth, so that if a particular guardian angel gained the ascendancy over his peers, the nation over which he had been appointed gained the ascendancy over the other nations of the earth. Thus, before a nation could be judged and punished, its angel ruler must first be dealt with. All such rulers, being subject to God's permissive will, would in the end be judged – like the nations over which they ruled. And so the key to terrestrial history is to be found in celestial event; history thus takes on a supramundane character; its meaning is to be found not only at the end of history, but also in the realm of spiritual being which is above history.

According to one tradition these guardian angels unfortunately overreached themselves and began to act independently of God, taking the control of the nations into their own hands. The writer of 1 Enoch, for example, tells of the seventy 'shepherds' or angels (according to Old Testament tradition there were seventy nations on earth) whom God had appointed to rule over the Gentiles but who overstepped their authority. They were told by God how many among Israel they were permitted to slay; but they slew many more than they were bidden and so would be thrown into the fiery abyss.

(e) 'Inferior angels'

Besides these superior or 'high-ranking' angels whom we have been considering – the elite of the heavenly hierarchy – there are innumerable 'inferior angels' commissioned by God to perform a whole variety of tasks. Some are set over the natural elements and are the spirits of thunder, lightning, sea, hoar-frost, hail, snow, mist, dew and rain (cf. I Enoch 60.11–24); others are 'leaders of the day and the night' and rule over the sun, the moon and the stars (cf. I Enoch 75.3). But to the popular imagination, the stars and other heavenly bodies do not simply represent the angel hosts (cf. I Enoch 80.6); they themselves assume the identity of angels, some of which fall from heaven (cf. I Enoch 86.1ff.) and as 'fallen angels' are judged and cast into the abyss (cf. I Enoch 88.1ff.). We recall in this connection the words of Revelation 1.20 where 'the angels of the seven churches' are represented as 'seven stars'. The imagery owes much to its Jewish background and, beyond that, to earlier

Persian and Babylonian belief, but its interpretation, like the stars themselves, is in the right hand of Christ.

3. WISDOM, SPIRIT AND LOGOS

(a) A comparative examination

The concept of Wisdom, which finds classic expression in such passages as Job 28 and Proverbs 8, is developed still further in Ben Sira 1.1ff.; 24.1ff., and in the Wisdom of Solomon 7.22ff. In the Proverbs passage it is presented as a female figure (the word is feminine in both Hebrew and Greek) who, according to the traditional rendering, stood beside God as his 'master workman' or 'clerk of works' at the creation of the heavens and the earth, helping him to lay its foundations (cf. 8.30). As such it has generally been taken as a personification of an attribute of God himself, the creator of all things. Gerhard von Rad, however, has argued cogently that the picture presented here is not that of a 'workman' but rather that of a 'favourite child' in whom God 'the father' delights. He points to the influence of Egyptian texts which speak of a 'darling child', Maat by name, who in Egyptian wisdom-teaching 'embodies law, world order, justice' (G. von Rad, *Wisdom in Israel*, 1972, p. 153). On this score Wisdom is not to be taken as an intermediary between God and his creation or as a personification of a divine attribute, but rather as a personification of that 'world order' or 'world reason' which gives meaning to God's creation. This is underlined by the fact that Wisdom herself, in the Proverbs passage, belongs to the creation-side for, as 8.22 puts it, 'The Lord created me at the beginning of his work, the first of his acts of old.'

This same thought of the 'creatureliness' of Wisdom is expressed in Ben Sira 1.1–10, where it is stated that God created Wisdom before all other created things and apportioned her to all his works. So too in chapter 24: in the beginning God created Wisdom; she sought a dwelling place among the nations and at last found it in Israel, ministering to God in his holy temple. Then, having extolled the works and manifestations of Wisdom, the writer says: 'All this is the book of the covenant of the Most High God, the law which Moses commanded us as an inheritance for the congregations of

Jacob' (24.28), i.e. Wisdom finds its supreme expression and embodiment in the Torah, which inculcates in men that 'fear of the Lord' which is the crown of Wisdom (cf. 1.18). This conviction no doubt reflected the experience of men like Ben Sira and the historical situation in which they found themselves, that obedience to the Lord should find expression in obedience to the Law (See ch. 4).

When we turn from the Hebraic Ben Sira to the Hellenistic Wisdom of Solomon we are at once aware of a marked change of emphasis, outlook and language. In particular the concept of Wisdom, which is developed still further in the latter, is deeply influenced by Greek thought and speculation. Building on the concept of Wisdom found in Proverbs as an 'order' or 'power' immanent in the world, he adopts the language and thought-form of the Stoic philosophers who spoke of a divine *dynamis* operative behind the many and diverse activities of creation. Von Rad comments that this author 'was the first to abandon, in this regard, the line which had been adhered to hitherto and take a decisive step along the road to a mythical, speculative deification of wisdom' (ibid, p.170). She is presented as a creator, a consort of God, a breath of the power of God, an emanation, a reflection of the invisible light, a spotless mirror of the divine mystery. She is not, however, a divine being alongside God. Though possessing many personal attributes, she is not a person as God is. She is rather a divine principle or presence through which God is seen and known by men, which pervades and penetrates all things and is a perfect revelation of God (cf. 7.22–8.1). This allusion to Wisdom pervading all things has reference to the world-soul or world-principle of Stoic belief by which all things are held together – an idea which elsewhere in the Wisdom literature is used with reference to the Spirit of the Lord (cf. 1.7) or the Word of God (cf. Ben Sira 43.26) and in the New Testament is related to the cosmic work of Christ (cf. Colossians 1.17; Hebrews 1.3). By so drawing on Stoic, and elsewhere on Platonic, language the writer of the Book of Wisdom was able to develop the concept of a power immanent in the world which had already found a pace in the Wisdom tradition of Proverbs 8 and was not altogether foreign to his readers. By such means the ancient biblical concept of Wisdom could be seen to be relevant to the Greek world in which they lived and become a vehicle for conveying the truth concerning the one, true and only God.

The writer of the Wisdom of Solomon is much more interested in the concept of Wisdom than in that of 'spirit'; but where 'spirit' does occur it is in close association with 'Wisdom'. Indeed in such a passage as 9.17 which alludes to the Stoic concept of 'spirit' permeating the universe and ordering all things in perfect wisdom, he virtually identifies the two: 'Who has heard thy counsel unless thou hast given wisdom and sent thy holy spirit from on high?'; i.e., the figure of Wisdom is so important to this writer that it must absorb into itself any other similar idea such as that of spirit and so stand supreme in its task of representing God to men.

But the advance towards what von Rad calls the 'deification of wisdom' had its severe limitations. The deep-seated Hebrew belief in the one god who is the Lord made it impossible for such a process to travel very far. This was made all the more plain by the concept of Wisdom itself which, as we have seen, is feminine in both Hebrew and Greek. It might be possible in Egypt to elevate Maat into a goddess, but this could not be done in Israel with Wisdom. It is true that in the Old Testament God's love is likened to that of a mother or a wife; but this is very different from saying that the God whom 'men worship as *He* should be known upon earth through a being whom they speak of as *She*' (L. H. Brockington, *Ideas of Mediation between God and Man in the Apocrypha*, Ethel M. Wood Lecture, 1962, p.16). The figure of Wisdom was a worthy representative of God, absorbing into itself not only 'spirit' but even the indescribable splendour and mystery of God's glory; but it was quite incapable of mediating the *person* of God. This is amply illustrated by the New Testament where Christ 'the one mediator between God and man' (1 Timothy 2.5) is presented as the power and the *wisdom* of God (cf. 1 Corinthians 1.24). His most characteristic mediatorial function, indeed, is not that of Wisdom at all but that of *Son* into whose hands the *Father* has committed all things.

Somewhat the same process can be traced in the case of yet another intermediary which had an even greater influence than Wisdom, at least for the development of *Christian* theology. This is the expression *Logos*, to be found in certain Jewish works of this period, and in which the influence of the Stoic philosophers is again evident. The most important of these for our purpose are the writings of the Jewish philosopher Philo (20 BC – AD 50) who saw in the Logos the supreme example of mediation between God and man, including the work of creation. As the world-permeating reason of God it can be called God's 'image' or 'his first-born son' or even 'the second God'. Such language, however, has to be taken figuratively, for Philo, unlike the Stoics, makes a clear distinction between God as initiator and Creator and the Logos as an expression, albeit supreme expression, of divine reason.

Complementary to this concept of Logos are certain 'powers' which correspond to Plato's 'ideas', through which God is seen to be everywhere present; these are the life-giving forces in the universe of which the Logos is the architect and enabler. These immaterial agencies serve as intermediaries between 'the intelligible world' and 'the world of sense and perception'.

The writer of the Wisdom of Solomon likewise makes use of this idea of 'Logos', linking it up closely with the 'Wisdom' of God, especially in the work of creation. For example, just as Wisdom sits on God's throne (cf. 9.4), so it can be said, 'Thine all-powerful Word (Logos) leaped from heaven out of the royal throne' (18.15). Or concerning creation: 'Thou hast made all things by thy word and by thy wisdom hast formed man' (9.1–2). No doubt we are to see here a reflection of that personification of Logos to be found later on in Philo; but we cannot overlook the fact that in the Old Testament the expression 'word' (Hebrew, *dabar*), when used with reference to God, is not to be understood in this way, but rather as an expression or 'extension' of God's will and action. It is true that, within Palestinian Judaism, in the Targumic use of the word 'memra' there was a tendency to personify the 'word' of God; nevertheless, even though personal attributes are given to it, the use is quite different from that of the Greek Logos, and expresses not personification so much as God's self-manifestation.

We conclude from this examination of Wisdom, Spirit and Logos not only that there is no equivalence in usage among these three terms, but also that for all practical purposes each of the three developments in religious thought which they represent follows its own independent course. It is true that Philo appears to identify all three, but even in this case Wisdom and the Spirit are shadowy figures with him as compared with the Logos. What we have in fact are three virtually independent theologies in each of which the tendency seems to be in the general direction of some form of 'binitarianism'.

(b) The early church's articulation

All three concepts were, of course, to a varying degree influential in the early church's articulation of its beliefs concerning the Godhead and in particular concerning the relationships of the persons of the Trinity. Nowhere do we find anything like a clearly defined doctrine of the Trinity in the New Testament, but the material is there ready to hand and such a doctrine is the inevitable outcome of what is recorded. The determining factor in the development of any such doctrine is undoubtedly the person of Jesus Christ with whom, for example, the *Spirit* of the Lord is so vitally related and who is, as we have seen, at least tentatively identified with *Wisdom*. But this latter concept is much less suitable than that of *Logos*, whose use is hinted at by Paul in Colossians 1.25–27 and again by the writer of Hebrews 1.1–3, but is most clearly set forth in the Prologue to John's Gospel. 'The author of the (Fourth) Gospel,' says J. D. Smart, 'had his own distinctive use of Logos, which embodied a critique of all contemporary usages' (*The Interpretation of Scripture*, 1961, p. 33). Here again the determining factor is seen to be the person of Jesus Christ as a fact of history. As in Philo, so in John, the Logos has a cosmological function; but the really important thing, says John, is that this Word became flesh and dwelt among us. The *ḥokmah-torah* (Wisdom-Law) figure of Judaism also has its parallel in the Fourth Gospel; but just as the Torah was given at a fixed point in time through Moses, so (says John) grace and truth came by Jesus Christ. And, of course, over and over again in Paul the relationship of the *Spirit* to the historical Jesus is emphasized. Just as there is one God who abides with men in the person of the Spirit, so there is 'one mediator between God and men, the man Christ Jesus' (1 Timothy 2.5).

VI

Demonology and the Problem of Evil

I. THE ORIGIN OF EVIL

The problem of evil in the world was one with which Hebrew writers had wrestled for generations. Not least had it held the attention of the wisdom writers who, in books like Proverbs, Job and Ecclesiastes, longed to believe in a perfect correspondence between the divine principles of justice and fair play in the universe and the expression of these things in their own relationships and experience. But experience belied belief, and the incidence of evil remained a mystery, to be accepted for what it was, without adequate explanation as to either its origin or its meaning, except that God himself was in it as both its cause and its cure (cf. Isaiah 45.7).

(a) Human freedom and divine control

In the literature of the intertestamental period, especially that of an apocalyptic kind, not only is the broad sweep of history predetermined (cf. II Baruch 48.3), even the thoughts of a man's heart are known beforehand by God (cf. Psalms of Solomon 14.5). Nothing that man can do can alter in any way what God has prescribed for him (cf. Psalm of Solomon 5.6). Even the future state of both the righteous and the wicked has been predestined by God (cf. II Baruch 42.7). Each man's path is set out before him and the heavenly tablets already contain the record of his judgment (cf. Jubilees 5.13).

Nevertheless, each man must take heed that he walks not in the way of transgressions lest judgment come upon him (cf. Jubilees 5.13). The course of a man's life, for good or bad, is a matter for that man's choice (cf. Psalms of Solomon 9.7). Each one enjoys free-will and knows when he is committing iniquity (cf. II Baruch 48.40). Just as Adam sinned, so each one is 'the Adam of his own soul' (II Baruch 54.19). In other words, the clash between predestination and free-will had not yet become a problem for these Jewish writers, so that these two apparently contradictory views could stand side by side without any obvious intellectual difficulty.

One popular account of the origin of human sinfulness illustrative of this tension is based on the Adam story as recorded in Gen. 3. In these books the writers look to the Paradise tale for a historical explanation and find it in Adam himself who is the primary source of sin (cf. II Baruch 18.2). That sin, however, is the cause only of physical death (cf. II Baruch 54.15); spiritually man is free to choose for himself. Sin can be traced back to Adam's fall (cf. Apocalypse of Abraham 26); nevertheless man is still responsible for his own sin (Apocalypse of Abraham 26). 'For though Adam first sinned and brought untimely death upon all, yet of those who were born from him each one of them has prepared for his own soul torment . . . and glories to come' (II Baruch 54.15). But it is noted elsewhere that Adam's sin has greater repercussions than these. He it is who is the cause of the perdition of the whole human race: 'O Adam, what have you done? Your sin was not your fall alone; it was ours also, the fall of all your descendants' (II Esdras 7.118). Indeed, through his sin the whole creation has become corrupted: 'When Adam transgressed my decrees the creation came under judgment' (II Esdras 7.11); compare with this the words of Paul in Romans 8.20 which describe how creation, having fallen away from perfection, 'was subjected to futility'. The very cosmos itself was deeply affected: 'Various cosmic disorders followed Adam's sin, the circulation of the planets was affected, wild beasts acquired their ferocity and obstinacy and lost their speech. . . The earth lost its fruitfulness, as did the trees, and the atmosphere ceased to be clear; while as for man, he lost the glory of his appearance, the eternity of his life, and the magnitude of his form' (W. D. Davies, *Paul and Rabbinic Judaism*, 1948, p.39).

The same tension between human freedom and divine control is illustrated in another theory, representative of the technical theology of the Rabbis, based on Gen. 6.5. This concerns the *yeṣer ha-ra'* or 'evil inclination' for which each man is responsible but which has been given by God. God gave it, but man is responsible for keeping it under control. According to the Rabbis it is not to be explained along hereditary lines; each person receives it at his birth or conception.

According to some apocalyptic writers, however, there is a 'good' inclination as well as an 'evil' inclination, so that 'if the soul takes pleasure in the good inclination all its actions are in righteousness . . . but if it inclines to the evil inclination all its actions are in wickedness' (Testament of Asher 1.6,8). This same thought is repeated in II Esdras where it is at least implied that the good and the evil inclinations lie side by side (cf. 3.21f.). The 'evil inclination' for this writer is described as 'the evil seed' (4.30) sown in the heart of Adam which expresses itself in 'the evil heart' (3.21) separating men from God (7.48). Adam's 'fall' was not his alone; it was also, as we have noted, the 'fall' of his descendants (cf. 7.118). In II Esdras, then, we seem to have a fusion of the 'Adam' theory of the 'fall' and the 'yeṣer' theory without a true synthesis being reached. Man is free to choose, but his infirmity is inveterate and he is 'clothed with the evil heart' (3.21f.).

(b) Fallen angels and evil spirits

A number of explanations are given in the literature of this period of the origin of evil which included, but far exceeded, sin in the human heart. Sometimes these are given separately; at other times the solution offered is of a composite character. The earlier books find the explanation in the story recorded in Genesis 6.1–4 which tells how the 'sons of God' (heavenly beings or angels) came down and took as their wives the comely daughters of men and bore children by them who grew up to be 'mighty men . . . men of renown'. This ancient story is taken up and embellished by the writer of I Enoch 6–36 and is repeated with variations on the same theme by other writers. In I Enoch 6, for example, these 'sons of God' are identified as two hundred angels, elsewhere called

'Watchers', under their leaders Azazel and Semjaza who lusted after the women, descended to earth and begat children by them. A variation is given in Jubilees 4.15 where it is said that they had been sent down by God himself to instruct men so that they should establish righteousness on the earth. Whatever the reason for their coming, the outcome of this illicit union was that corruption, bloodshed and lawlessness were spread abroad throughout the earth (cf. 1 Enoch 9.1); the depravity of the whole human race is to be traced back to this act of seduction. God acts in response to the cries of men; Azazel and Semjaza are bound until the final judgment when they will suffer torment and imprisonment for ever (cf. 1 Enoch 10.13). The children of the Watchers are destroyed 'because they have wronged mankind' (I Enoch 10.15).

These 'children of the Watchers' are described as 'great giants whose height was three thousand ells' who caused all kinds of evil to flourish in the earth (cf. I Enoch 7.3ff.; 8.1ff.). They are called 'evil spirits' for, when they die, evil spirits proceed from their bodies which 'afflict, oppress, destroy, attack, do battle and work destruction on the earth' (cf. I Enoch 15.8ff.). To them is due the corruption of all mankind. In the Book of Jubilees God orders them to be bound, but at the request of their leader Mastema he allows one tenth of them to remain at the beck and call of Satan (cf. 10.11).

Elsewhere in these writings the fallen angels are represented as stars. Enoch, for example, 'saw many stars descend and cast themselves down from heaven' (1 Enoch 86.3). On reaching earth they cohabit with the women who produce as offspring three kinds of giants which work much havoc on the earth (cf. 86.4ff.).

In the popular imagination, then, evil in its many and varied forms – in men, nations and nature – is to be traced back to the fallen angels and in particular to their evil progeny in the shape of demons or evil spirits which inhabit the earth and fill the air that people breathe. Such an interpretation of Genesis 6 was foreign to Old Testament thought and has much in common with the syncretistic Greek/Babylonian/Persian thought so prevalent at the time in which are to be found accounts of the mating of gods and women and the emergence of demons as the surviving spirits of supermen of a bygone age.

(c) Satan and his angels

There is another tradition, however, which traces back the origin of evil even before the fall of the angels from heaven. In the Similitudes of Enoch (1 Enoch 37–71), for example, it is traced back to a rebellion in heaven on the part of certain 'Satans' or evil spirits (for such they are), ruled over by a chief 'Satan' (cf. 53.3). They have free access to heaven and can stand in the presence of the Lord of Spirits (cf. 40.7). They have the task of accusing men; they tempt them to do evil and act as angels of punishment even against the 'Watchers' whom they bind with 'iron chains of immeasurable weight' (54.3). In II Enoch the chief of the rebellious angels is named as 'Satanail' (18.3) who is described as an archangel who set up his throne in the heavens and claimed equality with God himself (cf. 29.4). God cast him down together with certain 'Watchers' whom he had enticed. Some of these went down to earth and seduced the daughters of men (cf. 18.4) and subsequently were imprisoned beneath the earth (cf. 18.6f.).

In II Enoch and again in the Life of Adam and Eve Satanail is called 'the devil' and 'this Adversary'. He blames Adam for his expulsion from heaven and demands that Adam worship him. God hurls him down to the earth with his angels. There, in the Garden of Eden, he entices Eve, speaking through the mouth of the serpent.

Here again we have a very marked development away from the concept of evil and its origin to be found in the Old Testament. There the word 'Satan' appears in three fairly late passages: Job 1, Zechariah 3.1–9 and 1 Chronicles 21.1. In the first two of these it appears with the definite article and signifies simply 'the tester' or 'the adversary' who is presumably a member of God's 'heavenly council'. In the third passage it has become a proper name and indicates one who is an adversary of God himself who entices David to act contrary to the divine will. In the apocalyptic writings we have been considering, however, he emerges as a demon prince who leads a great army against the Almighty and is bent on wresting the rule from his hands. He or his henchmen are known by several names such as Asmodeus, Semjaza, Azazel, Mastema and Belial (or Beliar). Sometimes they indicate Satan himself. At other times they signify the leaders of his demonic host. But one thing is sure – the time will speedily come when Satan and his rebel angels will be judged and God will redeem the sons of men.

2. EVIL SPIRITS AND THEIR MANIFESTATIONS

(a) Corruption and disease

It is clear from a reading of the Jewish literature of the intertestamental period that the minds of the common people were preoccupied with the reality of demons and demon-possession to which were due the ills of mankind, and indeed of creation itself. As the writer of I Enoch puts it, 'The spirits of the giants afflict, oppress, destroy, attack, do battle, and work destruction on the earth, and cause trouble; they take no food, but nevertheless hunger and thirst, and cause offences. And these spirits shall rise up against the children of men and against the women, because they have proceeded from them' (15.11). In particular they will continue to incite men to sin right up to the day of final judgment (cf. 16.1). To them is due the corruption of all mankind. The same story is told in Jubilees which tells how the evil spirits urge men to wage war and to enslave their brothers (11.2ff.) and lead them on 'to do all manner of wrong and sin, and all manner of transgressions, to corrupt and destroy and to shed blood upon the earth' (11.5). Two demonic leaders are singled out for special mention: Azazel has 'taught all unrighteousness on earth and revealed the eternal secrets which were preserved in heaven' (I Enoch 9.6), and Mastema leads men astray from the way of God and sends forth his spirits 'to do all manner of wrong and sin' (Jubilees 11.5).

In particular, diseases and maladies of many kinds were believed to be the work of demons: 'the smashing of the embryo in the womb so that it may be crushed, the flagellation of the soul, snake bites, sunstrokes, the son of the serpent' (I Enoch 69.12). Josephus, writing of King Saul, also saw in the demons the cause of his disturbed and disturbing condition when David began to prophesy: 'He was beset by strange disorders and evil spirits which caused him such suffocation and strangling that the physician could devise no other remedy save to order search to be made for one with power to charm away spirits' (*Antiquities* VI. viii. 2).

For the treatment of such diseases and maladjustments traditional remedies were at hand. The physician's art in those days left much to be desired and his remedies were far from re-assuring. In Pliny's *Natural History*, for example, we are given lists of strange concoctions used in the West as remedies for all kinds of ills: 'the ashes of charred wolf's skull, the horns of a stag, heads of mice, eyes of crabs, owls' brains, salt of vipers, frogs' livers, locusts, bats, elephant lice, are the drugs with which the skilled physician worked; he even prescribed the gall of wild boars, horse's foam, woman's milk, the application of serpents' skins, the urine of calves which were unweaned, bears' grease, the extract of decocted buckshorn, and similar messes' (A. Hausrath, *A History of the New Testament Times*, 1878, vol. 1, p. 131).

Ben Sira had a much higher regard for the physician, however, than Pliny, holding him in honour and counselling his advice: 'Honour the physician with the honour due him, according to your need of him, for the Lord created him. . . The skill of the physician lifts up his head, and in the presence of great men he is admired. The Lord created medicines from the earth, and a sensible man will not despise them. . . The pharmacist makes of them a compound . . . and from him health is upon the face of the earth. . . Give the physician his place, for the Lord created him; let him not leave you, for there is need of him. There is a time when success lies in the hands of physicians' (38.1–4, 8, 12–13). Nor must the sick man neglect his own spiritual preparation in the process of healing: through prayer, repentance and the making of oblations he prepares the way for the physician's skills which are a gift from God (cf. 38.9ff.).

But in the popular imagination it is clear that disease and evil spirits went closely together and that relief and healing were to be found in the power of exorcism, in the exercise of which some men were specially gifted. Here we are introduced to a world of myth and magic in which incantations, gesticulations, mysterious oaths and secret formulae all have their part to play. Thus in the Book of Tobit the archangel Raphael bids Tobias 'take live ashes of perfume and lay upon them some of the heart and liver of a fish so as to make smoke. Then the demon will smell it and flee away and will never again return' (6.16f.). In the Book of Jubilees it is reported that Noah was taught the art of healing by the angels because of his resistance to the demons: 'And we explained to Noah all the medicines of their diseases, together with their seductions, how he might heal them with herbs of the earth. And Noah wrote down all things in a book as we instructed him concerning every kind of medicine' (10.12f.). This description recalls the secret books said to be used by the Essenes by which they learned the medicinal power of roots and the quality of stones.

In this connection we recall the strange account given by Josephus concerning the so-called 'Baaras root', from a place of that name, used effectively in exorcism. It is flame-coloured, he tells us, and towards evening emits a brilliant light. When an attempt is made to pluck it, it shrinks up and will remain still only when 'certain secretions of the human body' are poured over it. But even then it is fatal to touch it. One device is to tie a dog to it which then pulls it up, though the dog itself will die in the attempt. This root possesses one virtue for which it is highly prized: the demons which enter living people and kill them 'are promptly expelled by this root, if merely applied to the patients' (*Jewish War* VII. vi. 3). The same root is probably referred to elsewhere in Josephus in his account of 'Solomon's ring'. God, we are told, granted Solomon 'knowledge of the art used against demons for the benefit and healing of men. He also composed incantations by which illnesses are relieved, and left behind forms of exorcisms with which those possessed by demons drive them out, never to return'. He then describes how one of his own countrymen, Eleazar, in the presence of Vespasian, cured certain men possessed by evil spirits: 'He put to the nose of the possessed man a ring which had under its seal one of the roots prescribed by Solomon, and then, as the man smelled it, drew out the demon through his nostrils. . . Then, wishing to convince the bystanders and prove to them he had this power, Eleazar placed a cup or foot-basin full of water a little way off and commanded the demon, as it went out of the man, to overturn it and make known to the spectators that he had left the man' (*Antiquities* VIII. ii. 5).

The exorcism was performed, says Josephus, to the accompaniment of incantations. On other occasions we are told of the efficacy of certain gesticulations or manipulations of the hands (cf. *Jewish War* IV. viii. 3) or of the power of a sacred oath in which 'the hidden name' is mentioned, before which the demons tremble and through which 'the paths of men are preserved and their course is not destroyed' (I Enoch 69.13–21, 25).

We have come far, then, from the world of the Old Testament scriptures into a world in which evil spirits and demons play a big part in the thinking and experience of the masses of the people and in which esoteric teachings readily find root in the circles of 'the initiated'. How widespread these teachings were it is difficult to say; but it clear that they must have had a wider influence than simply the circulation of the writings that contain them.

(b) Cosmic control

This problem of disease and suffering, however, was only part of a much greater problem of evil which assumed *cosmic* proportions. The whole physical universe including the physical elements and the nations of the earth was in the control of rebellious forces who had spurned the rule of God and were bent on usurping his rightful place of authority. They had been placed in positions of trust by the Almighty, but now refused to take their orders from him. Instead, they had elected to serve their own self-appointed leaders and were drawn up in battle-array against God and all his 'angels of light'.

God, it was believed, had set guardian angels over the nations of the earth, thus forming a heavenly counterpart, as it were, of the Gentile rulers into whose power he had from time to time given his people Israel by reason of their sin. Wars on earth were paralleled by wars in heaven, so that the victory of a guardian angel marked the corresponding victory of the earthly ruler over whose nation he had been appointed. Both angelic and earthly rulers were answerable to God; but both had taken it upon themselves to rebel against him. Thus the key to terrestrial history, and in particular the suffering of the nation of Israel at the hands of the Gentiles, was to be found in celestial events. (For a fuller account of guardian angels of the nations, see D. S. Russell, *The Method and Message of Jewish Apocalyptic*, 1967, pp. 244ff.)

In Daniel 10.13ff. reference is made to a certain angelic 'prince', named as Michael, who is introduced as the guardian angel of Israel. He and another angel, probably to be identified with Gabriel, will join battle with 'the prince of Persia' on Israel's behalf and will lead their people to final triumph. In Jubilees 15.31f., however, it is said that God alone is Israel's guardian and that the angels who have been set over the nations have 'led them astray', as elsewhere the demons are said to have done (cf. 10.3, 8). In I Enoch 89.59ff. a related account is given of how God gives his people over, in the course of their long history, into the power of seventy 'shepherds'. He tells them how many of the people may be slain and how many spared; but the 'shepherds', representing no doubt angelic rulers, exceed their responsibilities and slay more than their allotted number, handing them over into the power of the Gentiles. Having overstepped their rightful authority they are declared guilty and are cast into the fiery abyss. In this way an explanation is given of the evil and suffering that had befallen Israel during its long and chequered history and in particular how it had 'received from the Lord's hand double for all her sins' (Isaiah 40.2).

Not only the nations, but the forces of nature themselves, were in the hands of angels or spirits (cf. Jubilees 2.2; I Enoch 75.3, etc.). The very stars in heaven were under their direct control (cf. II Enoch 4.1f.) and were popularly regarded as angelic beings in their own right, some of which as fallen angels fell from heaven (cf. I Enoch 86.1ff.). Not only the sin of man and the suffering of Israel, then, but also the corruption and alienation of the whole physical universe was due to the machinations of cosmic evil powers in the form of fallen angels and demonic agencies under the leadership of 'the prince of demons' Satan himself, or one or other of his demonic 'princes'.

All this is by the permissive will of God whose world has been usurped and whose people have been made to suffer beyond the limits set. Judgment will inevitably follow; the evil forces entrenched in the world will be destroyed, and God's creation will be restored to its original goodness. But none of this will happen without a struggle. 'The time will speedily come when there will be a "showdown" between the kingdom of God and the kingdom of Satan. This dramatic conflict between the *civitas dei* and the *civitas diaboli*, which has been going on from the beginning of the world and which has swept up into its toils men and beasts and all created things will reach its grand finale' (ibid., pp.271f.). 'Calamity,' says the writer of Jubilees, 'follows on calamity and tribulation on tribulation' (23.13). There will be fearful wars with nation rising against nation; earthquakes, famines and destruction by fire; fearful and mysterious portents will apear with no rational explanation. As the writer of Daniel puts it, 'There shall be a time of trouble, such as never was since there was a nation even to that same time' (12.1). The whole universe will be in a state of terrible conflict as the powers of light clash with the powers of darkness. But then will come the end. Satan and his armies will be defeated. His demon hosts will be routed. God's rule will be re-established. Creation, delivered from the tyranny of evil forces, will be re-created and Paradise will return on earth.

The redemption envisaged, like the conflict itself, is not one simply of sins forgiven and diseases cured; it involves the whole of God's creation, a cosmic redemption in which the universe itself is to be released from bondage and restored to its pristine beauty and original goodness. Earthly and heavenly, material and spiritual, history and eternity, men and angels, disease and demons – all are subject together to the powers of that kingdom which will know no end (cf. Dan. 7.14).

3. THE NEW TESTAMENT WITNESS

(a) Sin and Satan

In the New Testament man is presented as a sinner who is responsible for his own sin, for by his own wilful choice he has sought the meaning of his life and destiny apart from God. This, at least, is the argument of a passage such as Romans 1.18–32 (and indeed of the Epistle to the Romans as a whole) which follows carefully and critically the line of Genesis 3 with its account of Adam's 'fall' and his self-assertion to be like God. In Romans 7, moreover, where Paul describes his moral wrestling, we are probably to find a reference to 'the two impulses' of rabbinic concern and his struggle against the 'evil *yeṣer*' within.

It is of interest to observe that in these central passages dealing with the cause and outcome of sin no reference is made to Satan, and that in a passage like James 1.13–16 which describes the root of temptation, the full responsibility is placed on man himself. Despite this, however, there are numerous references in the New Testament to Satan and his demons as the cause of sin and all kinds of evil. Thus he appears under many names: the devil, the enemy, the evil one, the dragon, the old serpent, Beelzebul, Belial and the prince of this world. He is presented not just as an accuser or even a tempter; he is the rebellious destroyer of God's world who himself will be destroyed. In particular, he incites men to sin, as in the case of Judas (cf. John 13.27). But although 'Satan entered into Judas', Judas is still responsible for submitting to Satan's wiles.

(b) Satan's rule

Reference to a war in heaven and the fall of Satan and his angels is found clearly stated in Revelation 12.7ff. There he is described as the dragon, that ancient serpent, the devil and the deceiver of the whole world who is confronted by Michael and thrown down. The account is repeated in Jude, verses 6 and 9, who adds that he and his angels are kept 'in eternal chains'. It is to these malign angelic beings that Paul alludes in Ephesians 6.12 and elsewhere as 'principalities and powers' – angelic rulers of darkness and spiritual forces of evil in the heavenly sphere. Against these powers, which threaten to hold the souls and indeed the whole world in bondage, Christians must fight, knowing that Christ by his death and resurrection has already triumphed and is able to save. It was these self-same 'rulers of this age' who 'crucified the Lord of glory' (1 Corinthians 2.8), but in that very death by crucifixion Christ 'disarmed the principalities and powers' and made a public spectacle of them, triumphing over them in his cross (Colossians 2.15). This final victory over Satan and his angels is foreshadowed in the

ministry of Jesus and in that of the seventy disciples whom he sent
out on a mission. 'Even the devils,' they reported, 'are subject to
us in your name', to which Jesus replied, 'I saw Satan fall like
lightning from heaven' (Luke 10.17f.). Already, albeit in vision,
'his doom is writ'. Nothing that Satan will do can harm them (cf.
Luke 10.19).

(c) Jesus' mission

In the ministry of Jesus and his disciples, as in the Judaism of that
time, Satan, sin and sickness were closely associated with one
another. In this connection Geza Vermes draws attention to a
fragment from Qumran cave 4 known as the 'Prayer of Nabonidus'
which reads: 'I was afflicted with an evil ulcer for seven years . . .
and a *gazer* pardoned my sins. He was a Jew from among the
(children of Judah)'. The Aramaic word *gazer* probably means
'exorcist' or, as Vermes puts it, 'one who exorcises by decreeing
the expulsion of the devil' (*Jesus the Jew*, 1973, pp. 67f.).

In the story of the paralytic in Mark 2.2–12 and parallel passages
in Matthew (9.1–8) and Luke (5.17–26) Jesus claims the authority
both to forgive sins and to heal disease, and these two belong
together in the mission he undertook in God's name. In the eyes of
his followers, however, he was no ordinary wonder-worker, but
rather the Saviour from sin and death (cf. Matthew 1.21; Acts 5.31;
Philippians 3.20f.; Titus 2.13f., 3.4–7; II Timothy 1.10). He had
been sent by God that men might 'turn from darkness to light and
from the power of Satan to God, that they may receive forgiveness
of sins' (Acts 26.18), for 'through this man forgiveness of sins is
proclaimed' (Acts 13.38). To this end 'he became obedient unto
death, even death on a cross' (Philippians 2.8). Through his death
and resurrection Satan is defeated and sin forgiven.

But the 'salvation' Jesus brought was that of the whole person
from the power of Satan and the grip of disease. There is ample
evidence in the Synoptic Gospels that Jesus claimed and demonstrated powers of exorcism and, alongside these, powers also of
healing diseases. The distinction between these two is sometimes
difficult to make; but it is of interest to note that in the former case
he makes no use of magical rite or manipulation or esoteric

gesticulation or secret oath. He speaks simply and directly and the demon departs. Even in the case of healing (if this is to be distinguished at times from exorcism) he uses the familiar medium of touch or the laying on of hands and on one occasion the application of saliva (believed to have medicinal properties, cf. Mark 8.23ff.) without the extravagances of speech and movement that so often accompanied the acts of healers and 'holy men'.

In his ministry of exorcism and healing, as in that of his disciples whom he sent out on the same mission, Jesus believed that the powers of the coming kingdom were even then being released: 'If it is by the Spirit of God that I cast out demons, then the kingdom of God has come upon you' (Matthew 12.28). The strong man, to whom he refers in the controversy about Beelzebul, is already being plundered – in men's lives, in the realm of nature and in the final enemy, death itself; Satan is already on the way out! The kingdom of Satan has more than met its match in the kingdom of God!

But before the final day of reckoning there will be a time of war, the like of which the world has never known, when 'the powers of Heaven' will be shaken, cosmic catastrophes will take place and men will come out of their graves (cf. Matthew, 27.51ff.; Mark 13). The powers of evil will make their last desperate attempt to win the day. But with the death and resurrection of Jesus, the victory of God's kingdom is assured. Through him God has destroyed the power of death and with it the devil himself (cf. Hebrews 2.14) and all his legions.

The salvation that Christ brings is thus a cosmic redemption, involving not only the souls and bodies of men, but the whole creation, set free at last from the powers of Satan, sin and death. In this hope the early church lived; for its final realization in the Parousia of Christ they prayed – *Maranatha*, 'Come, Lord Jesus'.

VII

The Secret Tradition of Jewish Apocalyptic

I. THE SECRET TRADITION

During the intertestamental period there existed in Israel a secret tradition, generally associated with the Jewish apocalyptic writings, which for several centuries went underground, as it were, to emerge at a much later date in the esoteric teaching of the mediaeval Kabbalists. It did not entirely disappear from sight during those years, however, for here and there we see it coming to the surface not only in rabbinic Judaism (in the Mishnah, the Tosefta and the Midrashim), but also in the New Testament scriptures (in the Gospels, the Pauline Epistles and more especially the Book of Revelation).

The main stream of this tradition can be traced back into the biblical prophetic tradition in such books as Ezekiel, Deutero-Zechariah, Joel and Isaiah 24–27, but there were many tributaries, some of which had their rise in traditions and cultures in many respects different from those of the Old Testament.

(a) Made known to 'the wise'

It can be said to be secret in a double sense: first because of its subject-matter about which more will be said presently, and secondly by reason of the fact that it was channelled through a small élite, a spiritual aristocracy, as it were, who claimed special insights into the divine purposes and a special understanding of God's ways in the universe. The writer of II Baruch, for example, states clearly, 'Thou dost not reveal thy mysteries to many' (48.2–3), whilst the writers of Daniel and II Esdras (12.47f.) emphasize that they are to be made known only to the wise among God's people or to those who are ready or worthy to receive them. According to Josephus, such esoteric knowledge was claimed by the Essenes, who, among other things, were able to predict the future (cf. *Jewish War* II. viii. 6, 7, 12), and we know from the Dead Sea Scrolls that the Qumran Covenanters prided themselves in their esoteric doctrines, even recording certain of their writings in a secret code; these divine secrets, to be revealed to those who are upright and perfect, must on no account be disclosed to any but the fully initiated members of the sect.

Frequent reference is made in the Jewish apocalyptic writings to a set of people called 'the wise' whose task it is to interpret to 'the many' the things which they themselves have been privileged to see and hear so that 'the many' may in turn become wise. This close connection between esoteric knowledge and divine wisdom is found at least as early as the time of Ben Sira (*c.* 180 BC) who tells us, in what must surely be an autobiographical passage, that it was the privilege and responsibility of 'the wise man' who had studied in the school of wisdom to uncover her secrets to those who sought her illumination: 'He will seek out the wisdom of all the ancients, and will be occupied with prophecies; he will preserve the discourse of notable men and penetrate the subtleties of parables; he will seek out the hidden meanings of proverbs and be at home with the obscurities of parables' (39.1ff.). That is, by a careful study of the scriptures and ancient tradition, and by the help of the spirit of wisdom, he will uncover the mysteries of God.

(b) A divine mystery

This word 'mystery' or 'secret' is familiar to us from its occurrence in the Book of Daniel where, in its Aramaic form *raz* (a loan word from Persian), it occurs nine times and is translated in the Greek versions by the word *mysterion*. Its use in Daniel 2.27–30 is typical: 'No wise men, enchanters, magicians or astrologers can show to the king the mystery which the king has asked; but there is a God in heaven who reveals mysteries. . . Not because of any wisdom that I have more than all the living has this mystery been revealed to me, but in order that the interpretation may be made known to the king.' Both here and in the Qumran texts it occurs, together with the Hebrew equivalent *sod*, to signify a divine mystery whose interpretation has been given to a select few. This word 'interpretation' (Hebrew, *pesher*; Aramaic, *peshar*) is also found frequently in these writings and, like *raz*, is an important key word. Just as in the Scrolls the Teacher of Righteousness is enabled by God to give the true interpretation of God's mysteries (see pp. 45ff.), so the authors of Daniel and the other apocalyptic writings believe that the same insight and responsibility have been given to them. In each case this revelation of divine secrets is not made known by merely human wisdom; it requires the gift of divine wisdom for its interpretation. It is interesting to note that in the Book of Daniel, and in the only other occurrence of it in the Hebrew scriptures (Ecclesiastes 8.1) the word 'interpretation' (like the word *raz* itself) is again closely associated with the idea of wisdom. Throughout the apocalyptic books, then, the writer is presented not only as a prophet declaring the coming of God's kingdom, but also as a wise man uncovering the mysteries of God's mind.

(c) An 'open secret'

The word *mysterion* is, of course, not unfamiliar to the reader of the New Testament; indeed it appears there fairly prominently with several different shades of meaning, the most common of which is that of an 'open secret', a divine plan in the form of a mystery concealed by God, but now revealed to those chosen to be recipients of it. This revelation is made known by Jesus himself, not only in his teachings but also in his very person. In him and through him the 'mystery of the ages' is made known.

In this connection we may compare the words of Jesus to his disciples as recorded in Mark 4.11, and parallel passages, with the words of Ben Sira quoted earlier on. Those who come to Jesus asking the meaning of his parables are told: 'To you has been given the secret of the kingdom of God, but for those outside everything is in parables', i.e. according to these Gospel writers, Jesus is able to make known the secrets of the kingdom and chooses to do so to his select few, the inner circle of his disciples, in typically apocalyptic style. In developing this same thought, the Apostle Paul follows the example of Jewish apocalyptic writers by bringing together the notions of mystery and wisdom: 'Lest you be wise in your own conceits, I want you to understand this mystery, brethren' (Romans 11.25), and in the same letter refers to 'the mystery which was kept secret for long ages, but is now disclosed'. The nature of that mystery he fills out in Ephesians 3, describing it as 'the mystery made known to me by revelation . . . the plan of the mystery hidden for ages in God who created all things, that through the church the manifold wisdom of God . . . might now be made known to the principalities and powers in the heavenly places'. In Colossians 1.26–27 he goes further still and asserts that this divine mystery, 'hidden for ages and generations but now made manifest to his saints', is to be identified with 'Christ in you, the hope of glory'. Meanwhile, the mystery of God's purpose to be made known in Jesus as Son of Man and in his coming kingdom remains part of the 'messianic secret' which will one day be perfectly revealed.

2. APOCALYPTIC AS REVELATION

Many definitions of apocalyptic have been attempted, and many characteristics have been noted which apply to many, if not all, the writings which bear that name (see my *The Method and Message of Jewish Apocalyptic*, ch. IV). None is altogether satisfactory. I have referred to it as a style of literature which, by its esoteric approach, conveys a particular *mood* of thought and belief (ibid, p.105). We may go a bit further and say that it is a variegated attempt to disclose in writing certain divine secrets which have been made known by divine revelation and which uncover, for those who have eyes to see, the hidden mysteries of God in creation and the ordering of the universe, in the working out of the divine purpose in history and in the consummation of that purpose at 'the end of the days'.

Such revelations come, more often than not, in the form of dreams or visions or auditions or else as vivid journeys through heavenly places in which the writer, or the one in whose name he writes, is transported in spirit or in body into regions beyond the reach of man and shown mysteries far beyond human comprehension. At other times the revelation is mediated through an angel who interprets the divine secrets which may be shared with the initiated but otherwise kept locked up and private until 'the last days'. Whatever form the experience may have, its import remains the same: God has been pleased to uncover his mind and purpose to his chosen few by means of a divine revelation which cannot be gainsaid. As Daniel says, 'There is a God in heaven who reveals mysteries' (2.28). Such revelations carry with them the authority, the *imprimatur*, of God himself.

This experience on the part of the Jewish apocalyptists has something at least in common with the mystic and not least the Jewish mystic of later generations. Writing of these Jewish mystics, G. G. Scholem makes this comment:

> With no thought of denying revelation as a fact of history, the mystic still conceives the source of religious knowledge and experience which bursts forth from its own heart as being of equal importance for the conception of religious truth. In other words, instead of the one act of revelation, there is a constant repetition of this act. This new revelation, to himself or to his spiritual master, the mystic tries to link up with the sacred texts of the old; hence the new interpretation given to the canonical texts and sacred books of the great religions. To the mystic, the original act of revelation to the community . . . appears as something whose true meaning has yet to unfold itself; the secret revelation is to him the real and decisive one (*Major Trends in Jewish Mysticism*, 1955, p.9).

This comment on the Jewish mystics casts light on our understanding of the Jewish apocalyptists also and underlines three things which, in some measure at least, they have in common: the reality of personal experience in the reception of divine revelation, the importance of tradition and the authority of scripture and its interpretation.

(a) Arising from experience

As has just been said, many of the revelations recorded in the apocalyptic writings are said to be given in the form of visions, dreams and the like or by the agency of an angel. There can be little doubt, from the composite nature of many of these books and from the artificial composition of the visions themselves, that much of the language used in such descriptions represents a stereotyped literary convention, woodenly copied by successive writers. Nevertheless, there are indications that, in a number of cases at any rate, these writers believed themselves to be genuinely inspired and did in fact undergo a religious experience, comparable in some ways with that of the mystic, in which they entered into the experience they were describing and which they ascribed to the ancient worthy in whose name they wrote.

This is indicated, for example, in the *effects* which are said to accompany such visionary experiences. It is difficult to imagine that the detailed accounts that are given are added only for effect or as part of the furniture of literary convention. It is much more likely that they reflect the actual experiences of the writer himself, so apposite are they to his own circumstances and so real to his own understanding of the divine revelation imparted. Thus, Daniel's heart is troubled at the coming of a vision and he is left in a state of bewilderment and terror (Daniel 10.27); he is emotionally disturbed and even physically sick (7.28; 8.27); he becomes dumb and loses consciousness (10.15; 10.9). Ezra too falls down as dead in a trance-like state (II Esdras 10.30). Abraham, confronted by the fire and a voice 'like a voice of many waters' records his experiences in these words: 'And I desired to fall down upon the earth, and the high place on which we stood at one moment rose upright but at another rolled downwards' (Apocalypse of Abraham 18). Such descriptions argue strongly that, in such passages at least, they reflect the actual experience of dream, vision or trance of the apocalyptic writers themselves.

This conclusion finds confirmation in the *preparations* that are made for the reception of divine revelation. Prominent among these is the practice of fasting as demonstrated, for example, in Daniel, II Esdras, II Baruch and elsewhere where abstinence from food and drink frequently precedes the granting of a vision. So too with special foods or drinks or diets which prepare the recipient both physically and spiritually for the revelation that is to follow. Of interest in this connection is the final chapter of II Esdras (14.38ff.) which tells how, in response to Ezra's prayer for inspiration, he is bidden to drink 'a full cup, full as it were with water, but the colour of it was like fire. . . And when I had drunk, my heart poured forth understanding, wisdom grew in my breast, and my spirit retained its memory.' It was the cup of inspiration filled with the holy spirit. It seems likely that this is more than simply a picturesque way of saying he became inspired to do the tasks that awaited him. It is probable that we have here an indication of one practice among others whereby the recipient of divine revelation prepared himself to receive visions from on high.

The claim that personal experience lay behind visionary expression finds further support in the fact that many of the visions recorded arise out of meditation on the scriptures and have a distinct bearing on the times during which the writer is living. Christopher Rowland in his book *The Open Heaven* argues with copious illustrations 'that this use of scripture may not have been merely an artificial construction by the writer which has subsequently been given a visionary framework' (op. cit., p.217). In many cases the vision recorded may very well reflect the actual visionary experience of the writer arising out of his reflection on the scriptures, and not least on the divine promises in scripture, made known through the prophets, but not yet having reached fulfilment.

Of particular interest in this connection are the recorded visions of God seated on his heavenly throne, surrounded by his angelic hosts. There is good evidence to show that such visions draw their inspiration from Ezekiel 1, where the prophet sees a vision of God seated in his celestial chariot, surrounded by 'living creatures' of strange appearance. A case in point is I Enoch 14.8ff. which clearly reflects Ezekiel 1, but adds to it much detail of a speculative kind which no doubt reflected the thought of the writer's own day and the circle within which he lived and which was to have such an influence on Jewish mystical thought in future generations. The same influence is to be found in the New Testament, in Revelation 4, where again there is dependence on Ezekiel 1 but with differences in detail and emphasis which reflect the experience and circumstance of the writer who records his vision under divine inspiration.

This picture of the seer entering by means of vision into the presence of God and being shown there the divine secrets of heaven and earth recalls the Old Testament picture of the heavenly *sod* or council of Yahweh in which the prophet, together with the *bene 'elohim* or 'sons of God', is a witness of the secret counsels of the Most High (cf. Isaiah 6). Jeremiah has the same picture in mind when he admonishes the false prophets of his day saying, 'If they had stood in my council, then they would have proclaimed my words to my people' (23.22), for, as Amos puts it, 'Surely the Lord God does nothing, without revealing his secret to his servants the prophets' (3.7). This same idea may have been present in the mind of Ben Sira when he tells how the prophet Isaiah was given by God knowledge of the secrets of the end-time: 'By the spirit of might (i.e. by divine inspiration) he saw the last things . . . he revealed what was to occur at the end of time and the hidden things before they came to pass' (48.22ff.). Or again, in II Esdras 14.5 the writer can say of Moses, 'I told him many wonderous things, showed him the secrets of the times, declared to him the end of the seasons.' It is reasonable to deduce that such a statement is more than a description conjured up out of traditional material only, but rather reflects the actual experience of the apocalyptic writer himself who genuinely believed himself to be inspired by God and to have been shown by God divine secrets hidden from others but now disclosed as a direct and authoritative revelation from above. An interesting side-light on this is given in the Manual of Discipline, among the Dead Sea Scrolls, where it is said concerning the Qumran community, 'he has joined their *sod* with the sons of heaven into a unified congregation and a *sod* of saintly fabric' (1QS XI.8), i.e. the council of the community is brought into communion with the heavenly council of angels. In like manner, it may be said, the apocalyptists, as recipients of similar divine revelation, are made members of the same heavenly *sod* and inheritors of the marvellous mysteries of God.

This emphasis on the disclosures of divine secrets as direct revelation from God in the form of dreams, visions and the rest gives us a clue to the possible origins of apocalyptic in Judaism. Rowland ventures the guess that:

> If one is to take the claim to visionary experience seriously, the most likely origin for apocalyptic seems to be among those prophetic circles which continued after the Exile to maintain the validity of visions as a means of understanding God's will. . . The main similarity between such circles and apocalyptic is the claim to direct access to the divine secrets through revelation. In other words, it is the stand on behalf of the divine charisma as a continuing mode of revelation against attempts to reject such claims in favour of more indirect channels of communicating the divine will (*The Open Heaven*, p.246).

Reference has been made already to Revelation 4 and to the likelihood there of personal experience in the form of vision lying behind the explanations and interpretations which the writer gives to explain the disclosures made known to him of the divine mysteries. The same can be said of the contents of other chapters besides. Indeed, the experience of vision and the expression of its interpretation belong together as the vehicle of revelation just as in the case of Jewish apocalyptic that went before. But perhaps the most striking comment on this topic is given in II Corinthians 12.2–4, where the apostle Paul describes those 'visions and revelations of the Lord' that have come to him: 'I know a man in Christ who fourteen years ago was caught up to the third heaven – whether in the body or out of the body I do not know, God knows. And I know that this man was caught up into Paradise – whether in the body or out of the body I do not know, God knows – and he heard things that cannot be told, which man may not utter.' Paul was no apocalyptist; but in this visionary experience his reception of revelation and his introduction to the divine mysteries had much in common with theirs.

(b) Conveyed by long tradition

The revelation of divine secrets, however, had a greater authority for the apocalyptists than simply that of personal experience, however God-inspired it may have been. They were convinced that it was conveyed to them by means of a long tradition dating from time immemorial and that the secrets they were passing on had in fact been received by them from the ancient past. Despite their deeply personal involvement they were nevertheless conscious of the fact that they were not so much creators as they were inheritors of a rich and varied hidden tradition which was eminently worthy of preservation. There is, of course, more than an element of truth in this claim, for, although the form in which Jewish apocalyptic has come down to us is essentially literary, the ideas it contains had no doubt a pre-literary history and are the variegated deposit of a lengthy oral transmission. Tradition of this kind obviously did not grow up in a night; nor was it simply the product of the over-heated imaginations of a few highly-strung fanatics. In a number of respects, and not least in its mythological allusions, it contained much Hebrew lore which had been either neglected or rejected and had accordingly not found its way into the canonical scriptures.

An interesting commentary on this belief that they were inheritors of a long tradition is to be found in II Esdras 14 to which reference has already been made. Moses, we are told, received from God on Mount Sinai not only the Torah which he was to publish openly, but also a 'secret' tradition which he was to keep 'hidden'. 'These words publish openly, but these keep secret' (14.6). When Nebuchadnezzar, however, sacked Jerusalem in 587 BC both the 'open' books and the 'secret' books were destroyed by fire (14.21). And so God commanded Ezra the scribe, the 'second Moses', to restore what had been destroyed. Ezra prayed for the inspiration of the holy spirit in his task, set aside forty days (like Moses on Mount Sinai) and, with the help of five scribes, he dictated 'in characters which they knew not' (14.42). At the end of forty days the task was done and the revelation recorded in ninety-four books (14.44) containing the words of the Torah itself and, presumably, the apocalyptic tradition: 'The twenty-four books that thou has written publish, that the worthy and unworthy may read (therein); but the seventy books thou shalt keep, to deliver them to the wise among thy people' (14.45f.) Whether this secret tradition is meant to include the oral law, as some would argue, or else refers specifically to the apocalyptic tradition, it seems clear from the recurring emphasis on the word 'secret' that it is this latter which the writer has uppermost in his mind. Indeed the very reference to *seventy* hidden books may itself have had esoteric overtones, for the word *sod*, meaning 'secret' has the numerical value of 'seventy' ($s = 60$; o or *waw* $= 6$; $d = 4$) – a coincidence (if such it was) which would hardly escape the notice of the apocalyptic writer. Some support at least for this suggestion is found in the use of the word *sod* to indicate the number seventy in the much later Babylonian Talmud ('Erubin 65a). To the writer of this passage in II Esdras, it would appear, both Torah and the secret apocalyptic tradition went right back to Ezra and to Moses himself and were received by him as divine revelation. These 'hidden' books were 'the spring of understanding, the fountain of wisdom and the stream of knowledge' (14.47), of equal antiquity and equal authority with the oral law and claiming a place alongside the written Torah itself.

Two 'devices' are used in these writings to express this idea of belonging to ancient tradition. One is the phenomenon of pseudonymity by which the writer identifies himself with some ancient hero like Moses or Ezra or Enoch or Abraham or Daniel who represents the particular line of apocalyptic tradition in which the writer believes he himself stands. The impression given by a reading of these books is that this phenomenon was no mere literary device, even though the practice was fairly common in the Hellenistic world of the time; the writer conveys his message with conviction and with an authority not his own. He writes as if he was the transmitter rather than the author of what was now being recorded by him, passing on those 'secrets' which, like the oral tradition itself, had been passed on from generation to generation and had found their inspiration and origin in the renowned man of God in whose name he now wrote. Just as the oral tradition could be said to have its origin in Moses, the fountain-head of all law, and the wisdom tradition in Solomon, the source of all wisdom, and the psalmody tradition in David, the spring of all psalmody, so the apocalyptic tradition could be traced back to the patriarchs and heroes of old who lived close to God and had access to his divine will. This sense of 'oneness' with the ancient worthy and the 'genuineness' of the writer's standing in a long line of tradition would be strengthened if, as has just been argued, the visions and dreams through which the revelations came corresponded to actual personal experiences.

On this argument there would be no attempt at deception on the part of the apocalyptic writers. They were convinced that they wrote with authority and that that authority derived ultimately from the supposed writer and rested on the venerable age of the revelations contained in those writings that bore his name. In a similar way, the readers of such books would be expected to accept them as authoritative utterances of divine disclosures made known to the ancient seer which had been kept hidden for many generations but were now being revealed 'at the latter end of the days'.

We may note here that pseudonymous authorship is not a characteristic mark of the New Testament writings, although there may be reason to see II Peter in this light and possibly also the Pastoral Epistles. The likelihood is that here (as in the case of the Jewish apocalyptic writers) the aim was in no way to deceive, but rather to try and express what the actual authors felt Peter and Paul would have wanted to say in the circumstances in which the letters were written.

The case of the Book of Revelation is rather different. There is no reason to doubt that its author was in fact called John and that hence it is not a pseudonymous work at all. In this case we have an apocalyptic writer, strongly influenced though he is by Jewish thought, breaking with the Jewish practice of pseudonymous authorship in the case of apocalyptic books. The revelation he had received was not given through some figure in the distant past in whose name and on whose authority he writes, but by his risen and glorified Lord who speaks directly to him his divine revelation. For this reason there is no need for him to relate the past to the present by means of history told in the form of prophecy. The tradition in which he stands is altogether different: it is the tradition of God's mighty acts in history which culminate in the sending and exaltation of his only Son. He accordingly writes in his own name and declares at first hand 'the revelation of Jesus Christ which God gave him to show to his servants what must soon take place' (Rev. 1.1).

The second device is that of secret books which, it was believed, had been received by revelation in the distant past, hidden from sight for many generations and carefully preserved in a long line of secret tradition, to be revealed now at the end of time. They contained the secrets of all the ages and their consummation. The very fact that they were now being revealed was a clear indication that the end was at hand!

Belief in such secret writings was widespread in the Hellenistic world, and within Jewish apocalyptic itself several accounts are given. The book of Jubilees, for example, tells how the patriarch Enoch (who occupied a place of special intimacy with God) passed on the fruits of his knowledge and wisdom to Noah to whom he taught also the art of healing by means of herbs and every kind of medicine (10.12–13). Noah wrote down all these things in secret books which he passed on to his eldest son Shem (10.14). In due course they came into the hands of Abraham, who is thus represented as the renewer of these ancient secrets, and finally into the custody of Levi who is presented as the permanent guardian of the age-long tradition in which the author of Jubilees himself now stands. Similarly in I Enoch the patriarch commands Methuselah his son, 'Preserve the books from thy father's hands and (see) that thou deliver them to the generations of the world' (82.1). These secret books are to be handed down from generation to generation in various languages (104.11) until they come into the hands of that generation for whom they have been preserved (104.12). Till that time, says the author of II Enoch, though they are in the hands of mortal men, they are watched over by two of God's chosen angels (33.11f.).

Secret writings of this kind are also associated with the name of Moses. According to the Assumption of Moses he instructs Joshua in these words: 'Receive this writing that you may know how to preserve the books which I deliver to you; and you shall set them in order and anoint them with oil of cedar and put them away in earthen vessels in the place which he made from the beginning of the creation of the world' (1.16f.). They were to be preserved and hidden in this way until 'the Lord shall visit you in the consummation of the end of the days' (1.18).

We are reminded of the Essenes who, according to Josephus and

Philo, had their ancient secret writings, from a study of which they learned the art of medicine and the properties of roots. The Qumran Covenanters also emphasized the secret character of their writings which they copied and preserved in readiness for the time when God would visit his people at the End. It is just possible that we are to see the preservation of the scrolls at Qumran against this background in which case their storage in the Judaean caves may have had a much greater significance than simply that of preserving them from the ravages of Roman soldiers.

In the Book of Revelation we have no exact parallel concept, but here too the divine revelations are contained in secret scrolls, to be opened at the time of the approaching End. In chapter 5, for example, John sees a scroll containing an account of the world's destiny in which is written in detail God's plan for the future days that remain, preserved until 'the last time'. He weeps because there is no one fit to break the seals thereof and open the scroll. There is only one who is able to disclose God's plan for all the ages and set in motion his work of recreation: it is 'the Lion of the tribe of Judah' who is introduced as 'a Lamb standing, as though it had been slain' (5.5f.). The crucified and exalted Christ is the key to the world's destiny. He alone, through his death and resurrection and through his exaltation to God's right hand, is able to make known the secrets of all the ages and bring them to their consummation. As in the case of pseudonymous authorship so also in the case of secret books, the authority for what is written does not derive from some figure in the distant past, however honourable and revered he might be, but from the Son of God himself.

(c) Based on scripture

In the illustration given above concerning Ezra's dictation of the ninety-four books under the influence of the holy spirit (cf. II Esdras 14) we observed that twenty-four of these were the Old Testament books which were read openly in the synagogues and seventy were in all probability the 'secret' apocalyptic writings which were to be kept 'hidden' until the last days.

Both of these, like the oral tradition, were of supreme importance and carried divine authority, having been received by Moses himself as divine revelation. It was the prerogative of the apocalyptic seer not only to make known to 'the wise' the divine mysteries contained in these secret books, but also to interpret the scriptures themselves in the light of this secret revelation. As we have seen in chapter 3 above, the plain meaning of scripture was not its intended meaning; it was essentially a code which was now being broken for the first time. We have a hint of this in Ben Sira who, as a wise man, seeks out the hidden mysteries of God as they are concealed in the subtleties and obscurities of 'parables' (39.2). We have more than a hint of it in the Scrolls where the emphasis is on the interpretation of prophecy, as the commentary on Habakkuk, for example, clearly shows. But the Qumran Covenanters do not confine themselves to such portions of scripture; they 'must act according to the interpretation of the Torah' in which their fathers had been instructed (Dam. Doc. 4.8), for by their so doing God would reveal to them 'the hidden things in which Israel had gone astray' (3.14). The secret revelation gives the true interpretation of scripture itself; it unlocks the mysteries of holy writ. In particular, the apocalyptic writers examined the prophetic scriptures and more especially the predictive side of prophecy and saw these being fulfilled in their own day as confirmation that the End was at hand.

And so their private experience of dream, vision and the rest through which they shared in a rich tradition of revealed mysteries and by means of which they were able to discern the true meaning of scripture made the apocalyptists a force to be reckoned with in the developing religious life of the people of God. Despite the opposition of certain rabbinic teachers to the encroachment of esoteric mysteries on the territory of the Torah as the supreme vehicle of revelation, the 'mysteries of the Torah' (described later in the Talmud as 'the things spoken only in a whisper') continued to have a powerful fascination even within rabbinic Judaism. So too with the developing Christian church. The presence of the Book of Revelation in the New Testament canon, albeit after much debate, is an indication of the importance the early church assigned to the apocalyptic-type vision as a vehicle of revelation. This emphasis was continued and enlarged in subsequent years by the development of a specifically Christian apocalyptic tradition and the production of many apocalyptic writings.

3. THE CONTENT OF THE TRADITION

Apocalyptic, then, is about the revelation of divine mysteries, to be made known through visionary experience, through received tradition and through the message of scripture. But what are these 'mysteries' about? To that question three broad answers can be given. They concern the working out of the divine purpose in creation, in history and in 'the age to come'. Hence the pre-occupation of many of the apocalyptic writers with cosmology, historiography and eschatology.

(a) Creation

The apocalyptists were interested in the creation of the cosmos, in the movements of the heavenly bodies and in the changing seasons which these were believed to control. The subject of creation is dealt with at some length in the Book of Jubilees, for example. (especially ch. 2), which presents a cosmogony, based on the twenty-two letters of the Hebrew alphabet. There the world is pictured in three tiers – the heavens where God dwells together with the angelic host, the earth with its waters, and what it calls 'the abysses and the darkness'. The earth itself is divided into three continents – Asia from the Nile (here called Gihon) eastwards and northwards to the river Don (here called the Tina), North Africa (here called 'Afra) from the Nile westwards to the Atlantic (here called 'Atĕl) and the sea of Ma'uk (probably a corruption of *Me okeanos*, the Great Ocean), and Europe from the Don westwards to the Great Ocean 'west of Fara' (presumably Africa) where it faces Gibraltar (such a division is in perfect agreement with that of Hecateus of Miletus and shows the influence of Greek thought on a book which purports to be strictly Jewish in origin and outlook).

But the apocalyptic literature as a whole is interested not so much in the work of creation as it is in its order and governance. That is, it is less concerned about cosmogony than it is about cosmology and the related subject, astrology, for therein the mysteries of God are revealed. By means of vision, dream and trance the seer is able to enter into the secrets of the universe which are normally hidden from mortal sense. Hints of this are given by the author of the Wisdom of Solomon who tells us that among those mysteries to be revealed are knowledge of the structure of the physical universe, the movement of the heavenly bodies and acquaintance with seasonal changes (cf. 7.17ff.). Or, as Ben Sira remarks, 'Many things greater than these lie hidden, for we have seen but few of his works' (43.32). Such mysteries are the subject of speculation in book after book in the apocalyptic literature, more especially in I Enoch and II Baruch and, to a lesser extent, in the Qumran texts. Some of this cosmic speculation has to do with the calendar and the task of fixing dates for religious festivals over which meticulous care was taken. One illustration of this is to be found in the so-called Book of the Heavenly Luminaries in I Enoch 72–82 which deals specifically with the laws of the heavenly bodies and their bearing on calendrical calculations. Reference is made in this same writing and elsewhere to the signs of the Zodiac which are in the control of the angels and are believed to control the destinies of men. Such thinking influenced even such strict Jews as those in the Qumran sect among whose writings there has been found an astrological cryptic document referring to a man born under the sign of Taurus the Bull.

In certain other passages, however, these cosmic mysteries are associated with moral and religious values which constitute part of the secret. Thus in I Enoch 71.3f. 'all the secrets of the ends of the earth' are described as 'the secrets of righteousness'. Such cosmic mysteries are a revelation of the righteous will of God who reveals them to the enlightened among his people (cf. 43.4), but not to sinners who end up by worshipping the stars as gods (cf. 80.7). In similar vein the writer of the first Qumran hymn, having recounted God's ordering of the heavenly luminaries and all the elements, concludes with these words: 'Thou has unstopped my ears to marvellous mysteries . . . but the foolish of heart shall not comprehend these things.' A knowledge of these mysteries of God in creation, which are at one and the same time orderly and righteous, enables men to understand his true nature. Failure so to discern leads to idolatry and sin.

Closely related to this interest in cosmology, and hardly separable from it, is the interest in theosophy. An allusion to this is no doubt to be found in a remark of Philo concerning the Essenes that they 'abandoned . . . metaphysics to visionary praters', focussing their attention rather on 'the existence of God and the creation of the universe' (*Quod Omnis probus liber sit* XII. 80). Particular attention is given by the visionary-apocalyptists to two mystical doctrines which in later times were to play a prominent part in Jewish theological and metaphysical debate. These are the *Ma'aseh Bereshit* ('In the beginning') based on the creation narrative of Genesis 1, and the *Merkabah* ('chariot') based on the description of the chariot described in Ezekiel 1, concerning which the Mishnah gives the injunction 'not to expound the chapter of Genesis before more than one hearer nor that of the heavenly chariot to any but a man of wisdom and profound understanding' (Hagigah 2.1).

The earliest reference to the Merkabah in this literature is in I Enoch 14, which tells how the patriarch is transported in vision to heaven: 'And I looked and saw therein a lofty throne: its appearance was as crystal, and the wheels thereof as the shining sun. . . And the Great Glory sat thereon, and his raimant shone more brightly than the sun and was whiter than any snow' (14.18ff.). Elsewhere this speculation is taken further and we find 'the living creatures' and even the wheels of Ezekiel's chariot transformed into angels 'who sleep not and guard the throne of his glory' (71.7; cf. 61.10). Such passages recall the vivid descriptions in the Book of Revelation of the throne of God which the seer was privileged to behold through an open door in heaven: 'He who sat there appeared like jasper and cornelian, and round the throne was a rainbow that looked like emerald' (4.3), or the 'great white throne' from which God would judge the world (20.11).

In the Similitudes of Enoch, moreover, strange and obscure names are given to the God who sits upon the throne and to his holy angels. Special power is acquired by those who have knowledge of their secret meaning, especially when used in an oath. Thus in 69.14 mention is made of 'the oath Akae' which is described as

116

'the hidden name . . . powerful and strong' and may, it has been suggested, be some secret representation of the Tetragrammaton. The mysteries of God, then, are to be found not only in creation itself but also in the very being of God in the knowledge of whose name there is life and power.

(b) History

A cursory reading of these writings might easily give the impression that the apocalyptists had little or no interest in history for its own sake, but only in the end of history when, by the miraculous intervention of God, all wrongs would be set right. This impression is reinforced by the phenomenon of pseudonymity which casts history in the form of prophecy and prediction, leading up to the End. Such an impression, however, is misleading and does less than justice to the fact that these writings were in a sense 'tracts for the times' in which the writers were then living and took very seriously indeed not only the historical events of their own day, but also all the generations that had gone before.

It is true that what the apocalyptists were primarily interested in was the movement of history towards its final goal in 'the new age' or 'the kingdom' or 'the age to come'. But for this very reason they took history seriously as the arena of God's activity in which and through which the secrets of his divine purpose for humankind were to be revealed. There was reason for them to despair if they were to look at the sufferings of their people only through human eyes. But as men who had been allowed to enter into the mysteries of God's working in the world, they were able to see the working out of the divine purpose from a divine perspective. This made clear that they had not been abandoned by God; his sovereign rule was supreme, despite many appearances to the contrary. The very fact that the long history of God's people demonstrated his care over them carried its own assurance that he would be there at the End to justify them in the sight of the nations. The secrets of his ways to be found in creation were to be found also in history for those who had eyes to see and wisdom to understand. The creation of the physical universe and the history of the human race alike were demonstrations of the sovereign power of God who, at his appointed time and in his appointed way, would bring in the kingdom.

The picture presented here is an impressive one, for it shows history as a unity, a totality, in which past, present and future are viewed in one continuous perspective. The Old Testament prophets had pioneered the way in this regard, but it is to the credit of the apocalyptists that they advanced much further the conviction of the divine purpose as the unifying principle of all human history. This applied not only to God's care of Israel, but also to his control of all the nations of the earth. The nations might rage, and God's people might suffer grievously at their hands; but as in the past so now in the present he is in control and will make his purpose in history plain in the very near future when his reign will begin. Nebuchadnezzer's dream-image representing four great world empires will soon be smashed to pieces by a stone 'cut without hands' which becomes a great mountain and fills all the earth (cf. Dan. 2.34f.). The kingdom of God will speedily replace the kingdoms of this world, and he will reign supreme. The whole of history testifies to this fact. Rowland compares the apocalyptists' view of history to 'a play with many scenes which have been written but not all acted out on stage. . . The apocalyptic seer is privileged to have a total view of the play, including that which is still to be actualized on the stage of history' (*The Open Heaven*, p.144).

But the apocalyptists went further than the prophets in their presentation of history as a unity in which and through which God's sovereign purpose was revealed. At the same time they divided it systematically into great epochs, each of which was determined by the sovereign will of God. In II Esdras 14.5 a hint is given of a secret tradition regarding the crises of world history associated with the name of Moses: 'I told him many wondrous things, showed him the secrets of the times, declared to him the ends of the seasons.' This tradition is spelt out in Jubilees and the Assumption of Moses, where the jubilee is used as a measurement of world history, and in the Apocalypse of Weeks in I Enoch (93.1–10; 91.13–17), where the history of the world is divided into ten 'weeks' of unequal lengths, seven of which have already passed.

But the mysteries of God are to be discovered not just in what we would call 'the historical process', but also and especially in that supra-mundane world, the heavenly places, where God dwells with all his holy angels. Between these two realms of 'history' and 'above-history', as we shall see more fully in chapter 8, there is a direct correspondence. Or, to put it another way, the events of history have a transcendent dimension in terms of which they are to be understood. Thus, as we have seen, in the Book of Daniel the nations of the earth are said to have their own guardian angels who fight on their behalf in the heavenly places (cf. Dan. 10.20f.); their victories or defeats are reflected in the varying fortunes of the nations themselves. Or again, as we have also seen, the council of the Qumran community could think of itself as 'a unified congregation' with 'the sons of heaven' (1QS XI.8). The earthly and the heavenly are, as it were, merged into one.

The apocalyptist, by means of the revelation granted to him, is able to read the pages of history in the light of its heavenly counterpart and to understand those secrets which can be known in no other way. To know the one is to know the other. But such knowledge of the heavenly mysteries holds the key not only to the past and present; it opens the door also to the future. Thus historiography opens up into eschatology as mysteries are unveiled of the working out of God's sovereign purpose in 'the age to come'.

(c) 'The age to come'

All the signs point to the control of God over the ordering of creation and the movements of history alike and give the assurance that the time is speedily coming when his sovereign will will be recognized in an act of re-creation and redemption when corruption will give way to incorruption and evil will be utterly destroyed.

What the creator willed and planned at the time of creation will reach its fulfilment in the last days; he will rectify and restore what has gone wrong and bring to perfection what he has made. The end will be as the beginning (cf. Rev. 2.7) and Paradise will be restored. More often than not the writers have in mind an earthly state in which earthly delights mingle with spiritual blessings. In some of the later books, however, the picture becomes transcendent in character and what is envisaged is 'a new heaven and a new earth', a spiritual realm which will form 'a new creation'. According to the Jewish Sibylline Oracles the earth will be destroyed by 'fire and cataclysm of rain' and 'brimstone from heaven.' The anger of God's judgment, says the Life of Adam and Eve, will show itself 'first by water, the second time by fire' (cf. II Peter 3.10ff.). By whatever means these things were to be brought about, the apocalyptic writers viewed creation itself as sharing in God's redemption – a belief expressed by Paul in his letter to the Romans: 'The creation itself will be set free from its bondage to decay . . . groaning in travail until now' (8.21f.). The whole created universe will at last reach its glorious fulfilment in the purpose of God.

Now, this picture of a cleansed and re-created universe is closely linked with the defeat of evil and the powers of evil entrenched within it (see chapter 6). The day will come when wicked men and demons will be judged and the whole universe will be cleansed and restored. In 'the mystery to come,' writes the author of the Qumran Book of Mysteries, '. . . wickedness shall retire before righteousness as darkness retires before the light and as smoke vanishes and is no more; so shall wickedness vanish for ever and righteousness appear like the sun.' In the great eschatological battle described in the War Scroll these words are to be inscribed on 'the trumpets of ambush': 'Mysteries of God for the destruction of wickedness.' Evil will be done away and righteousness will remain supreme. The holy and righteous purpose of God will at last be vindicated. 'Splendid in every secret thing is thy power,' says Enoch, 'from generation to generation, and thy glory for ever and ever; deep are all thy secrets and innumerable, and thy righteousness is beyond reckoning' (1 Enoch 63.3).

But before these things come to pass, there will be a period of unprecedented 'woes' when the powers of evil will make their last desperate attempt to overthrow the powers of good. They will launch their attack on God's people and on God's whole universe. The name sometimes given in later Jewish and Christian writings to this period of distress before God's final triumph is 'travail pains of the Messiah'. With this we may compare Mark 13, whose listed 'woes' are described as 'the beginnings of the birth pangs', or Revelation 12.1–6, where the birth of the Messiah or the messianic community from the womb of the true Israel is likened to a woman who 'crieth out, travailing in birth, and in pain to be delivered' (12.2), or the Qumran Hymn III, 7–10 which uses the same metaphor to the same end. Even the physical universe itself will be affected: the world will be stricken by earthquake, famine and fire; there will be mysterious portents on the earth and in the heavens reminding men that the End is near.

Closely associated with these 'signs of the end' is the figure of Antichrist who, it was believed, would appear in the last days to do battle with God himself. The actual term first appears in Christian writings and is reflected in the 'Man of Sin' in II Thessalonians 2.3; but the idea is vey much older and reflects a well-established legend familiar to the writers of these apocalyptic books. Sometimes he appears as a human being and at other times as an embodiment of Beliar himself, the prince of demons.

In these books there is a bewildering variety of eschatological expectations. As we shall see in the final chapter, the rule of God is sometimes presented as a permanent kingdom here on this earth, purified and restored or else entirely re-created. At other times it appears as a temporary kingdom on earth, to be replaced by 'the age to come'. At other times again it seems to be an entirely transcendent realm where men and angels share together in eternal bliss. Sometimes the outlook is nationalistic: God redeems 'the righteous' and his judgment falls on 'the wicked' who will rise in resurrection to receive the due rewards of their deeds. No longer are God's enemies confined to men of flesh and blood; they are the cosmic powers of darkness. Thus, in some of the apocalyptic writings at least, an eschatology emerges which, in the words of Mowinckel is at once 'dualistic, cosmic, universalistic, transcendental and individualistic' (S. Mowinckel, *He that Cometh*, 1959, p.271).

VIII

The Future Hope

I. THE CONSUMMATION

(a) The 'messianic' kingdom

A confident expectation on the part of many in Israel at this time was the hope in a coming messianic kingdom which would put an end to their miseries and usher in a new era of righteousness, security and peace. It was intolerable that evil should prevail and triumph in the end. The troubles through which they were passing were but harbingers of the kingdom. These very 'messianic woes' were as birth-pangs before the birth of the kingdom. Like the broad sweep of history, these 'woes' were also in the hands of God and subject to his sovereign will.

The conviction was widespread, moreover, not only that the kingdom was coming, but that it was coming soon. Some waited with patience and gave themselves to the study of the Law in which God's mind was revealed. Their living under the yoke of the Gentiles was a direct result of their sinning against God. By fulfilment of the Law and by repentance they would turn aside God's anger and hasten the coming of the kingdom. And so we observe the growth and spread not only of Torah-study, but also of many baptizing groups in Palestine and beyond calling for repentance that the dawning of the kingdom might appear. Others waited with impatience and gave themselves rather to force of arms and rebellion which found focus in AD 6 in the birth of the Zealot movement, pledged to rid Israel of its Roman foes and thus help to bring in the kingdom. Others again, by the interpretation and re-interpretation of scripture, sought to calculate and forecast the exact time of its appearing. Thus, the seventy years' captivity forecast by Jeremiah (cf. 25.11–12; 29.10) are taken by the writer of Daniel to signify 'seventy weeks of years' and are made to refer to 'the time of the end' which, according to his calculations, coincides with the day in which he himself is then living! This method of working is only one illustration of the fascination which sacred or secret numbers had for many at this time. But, however mistaken their calculations may have proved to be, the conviction remained that the kingdom would come and that the end was close at hand.

Concerning the character and fruits of this coming kingdom, there is no complete consistency in the writings of this period. Certain general observations, however, may be made. The power of the Gentiles will be curbed: they will be forced to pay homage to Israel or else will be utterly destroyed. The people of God 'whose delight is in the Law of the Lord' will be vindicated and their tribes gathered together to Jerusalem. Israel itself will be purified, the ungodly will be judged and God himself will reign in righteousness.

For the most part the kingdom will be established here on this earth or else on a renewed earth or, in a few cases, in a new transcendent order. In the Book of Daniel, for example, it belongs to this earth and is of the very stuff of history (cf. 7.13f.). Its blessings are material as well as spiritual; its inauguration marks the fulfilment of political as well as religious aspirations. It is a universal kingdom in which the dominion of the Gentiles is transferred to Israel; it is an everlasting kingdom which will never be destroyed or given to another; its coming is imminent; and the rightous dead will be raised in resurrection to share in its blessings. So, too, in the Psalms of Solomon, for example, dating from the first century BC, the kingdom is established on earth with the help of a militant Messiah who will subdue his Gentile foes.

But already the picture of this earthly kingdom is beginning to be idealized, as in I Enoch 6–36, where it is presented as some kind of Golden Age in which the earth will be cleansed of all oppression, the soil will produce marvellous crops and the righteous will beget thousands of children (cf. 10.17ff.). The location of such blessings, however, is still this earth, albeit transformed and renewed.

In some of the later pseudepigraphical writings, however, as in the rabbinic sources, a clear distinction is made between the messianic kingdom, which is regarded as temporal and provisional, and an eternal future age which takes on transcendent qualities and, in certain instances, represents a new order of being altogether in an other-worldly, timeless eternity.

In the so-called 'Apocalypse of Weeks' for example, contained in I Enoch 91–105, as we have already seen, world history is divided into ten 'weeks', seven of which are almost past. At the beginning of the eighth week the messianic kingdom will appear and continue until the tenth week during which sin is banished from the earth. Then is introduced the age to come, a time of reward and punishment, when the righteous will shine as 'the lights of heaven' and the wicked in Sheol will be 'wretched in their great tribulation'.

In II Enoch it is said that world-history will run for 6,000 years, to be followed by a 'rest' of 1,000 years during which God will establish his kingdom. The wicked will be judged and the righteous will be raised in 'spiritual bodies' to live in Paradise 'between corruptibility and incorruptibility' (8.6). In II Baruch it is said that the kingdom will be established on a renewed earth and will continue 'until the world of corruption is at an end' (40.3). It is the prelude to 'the new world which does not turn to corruption those who depart to its blessedness' (44.12). The dead are raised and enter into 'the world which does not die' (51.5) where they will live a life free from evil in a world which does not age (51.16).

Again, in II Esdras the kingdom, which is set up on earth, is to last for 400 years (7.28) and is for the surviving righteous only. At its close there will be seven days of primaeval silence at the end of which 'the age which is not yet awake shall be roused, and that which is corruptible shall perish' (7.31). There will then follow a general resurrection and all men will be judged, confronted by 'the furnace of Gehenna' and 'the Paradise of delight' (7.36).

A variation on this theme of temporary kingdom followed by age to come is given in the Book of Revelation. There a millennium is introduced during which Satan is bound and in which the saints share by resurrection. At the end of the thousand years Satan is loosed and attacks the saints, only to be cast into the lake of fire (cf. 20.1–10). A general resurrection and final judgment follow. Then is set up an everlasting kingdom in a new Jerusalem.

We find, then, in these writings (particulaly dating from the first Christian century) suggestions of a dualistic view of the world in which 'this age' of sin, corruption and oppression is set over against 'the age to come' in which evil will be destroyed and righteousness will be vindicated once and for all. As the writer of II Esdras succinctly puts it: 'The Most High has not made one age but two' (7.50). But although such a belief had a profound influence on later Jewish and Christian thinking, it was not typical of the majority of Jewish writings during the intertestamental period, which continued to view this earth, however defined, as the sphere of God's coming redemption.

(b) Messiah and Son of Man

So far we have been using the expression 'messianic kingdom' to describe the coming time of deliverance when God will vindicate his people. This title, however, can be misleading and requires a clear understanding of the concept 'messianic' in this context.

In the Old Testament the Hebrew word *mašiaḥ* (Greek, *messias*), meaning 'anointed', does not have the technical meaning of 'Messiah' which it comes to have in later Jewish and New Testament writings. With the definite article it simply signifies 'the anointed one' and generally refers to the king of Israel and in particular the Davidic line, i.e. it indicates an earthly, human, historical king.

Now, in the Old Testament we have a number of so-called 'messianic prophecies' describing the coming of a golden age when God will establish his kingdom of justice and peace and vindicate his people. In some of these, though not all, reference is made to an ideal king who will rule over this coming kingdom as God's own representative. But it is to be noted that nowhere in these prophecies is he given the title 'Messiah'. Thus in some of these 'messianic prophecies' we have a promised kingdom in which God alone is king, and in others we have an ideal king who is not called 'Messiah'.

When we come to the intertestamental period we find the same hopes very much alive. A case in point is the Book of Daniel where, however, in common with several other apocalyptic writings no specific reference is made to a Messiah. But in other writings and in the popular expectation of the people, as we have seen, there was a growing expectation of a coming deliverer of David's line who would establish his kingdom. Of significance in this connection are the Psalms of Solomon, written about the middle of the first century BC, for there, for the first time in the literature of this period, the technical name 'Messiah' is used as a title of the coming king. This deliverer, we note, will be a king of David's line, i.e. a thoroughly human being who will fight for the cause of his people Israel and set up his kingdom on earth with Jerusalem as its centre. But his moral and spiritual qualities are singled out for special mention. God will equip him with everything he needs; he will rule in righteousness and wisdom and will himself be free from sin.

Somewhat earlier on the hope had been expressed by some, including it would seem the Qumran Covenanters, that God would provide a priestly Messiah alongside a kingly Messiah. But the popular hope remained that in God's good time the 'son of David' would arise to save his people and establish his kingdom.

Alongside this tradition of the Messiah as a kingly deliverer there went another tradition, soon to be intertwined with the first, of the Son of Man as a heavenly saviour. The beginnings of the tradition are to be found in Daniel 7.13ff. which describes how 'one like unto a son of man' comes with the clouds of heaven and is presented to 'the ancient of days'. This figure is not introduced as the Messiah, but is identified in 7.18 as 'the saints of the Most High', to whom will be given a kingdom that will not be destroyed. Just as the four beasts in the vision represent four kings or kingdoms, so the 'son of man' represents Israel.

Some scholars, however, see in this Son of Man 'the beginnings of a belief in a heavenly saviour-figure which contributes to the developing belief in a supernatural messiah in Jewish religion' (Christopher Rowland, *The Open Heaven*, 1982, p.178). The Son of Man, it is suggested, is perhaps to be identified with the archangel Gabriel. What happens to him in the heavenly places is paralleled, as it were, with what happens to 'the saints of the Most High' here on earth. Just as he is given dominion, so they are given dominion over the kings of the earth.

This same idea of a heavenly Son of Man is taken up and developed in the Similitudes of Enoch (I Enoch 37–71) where he is identified with Enoch himself. A second title, 'the Elect One', is also used. He is presented as a heavenly being whose face is 'full of graciousness, like one of the holy angels' (46.1). He himself is not pre-existent; but his 'name' was known by God 'before the stars of heaven were made' (48.3). All the secrets of the universe are hidden with him (52.1ff.) and the greatest secret of all is the Son of Man himself who, though now hidden, will one day be revealed (48.7). Then he will appear in all his splendour to be the judge of heaven and earth, of men and angels (61.8), and the righteous will share in his kingdom (61.5).

The relation between the Son of Man and the Messiah has been a subject of much debate among scholars. Two things are to be noted in this connection: one is that this transcendent figure is described at times in terms reminiscent of the traditional under-standing of the Messiah – he is righteous and wise, he receives the homage of kings, he is a light to the Gentiles and so forth; the second is that on two occasions he is described as 'the anointed one' of God (cf. 48.10; 52.4). Whether this is to be taken as simply a description or as a technical title, it is significant that as early on as this (possibly late first century BC) the title 'Son of Man' is placed in a 'messianic' setting.

Another passage of some importance for the development of the Son of Man concept is II Esdras 13 (c. AD 100). He is presented here as a pre-existent, transcendent figure who will appear before the righteous in all his glory. Everything about him is secret; but when his time arrives he will come on the clouds of heaven; he will then sit on God's glorious throne and all that is hidden will at last be revealed. This majestic figure is identified with the Messiah, being called 'my Messiah' and 'my son the Messiah' (7.28f.) who 'shall spring from the seed of David' (12.32). This Messiah, we are told, will effect justice and deliverance and, at the close of the interim kingdom over which he rules, will die as other men die (7.29). This, then, is no suffering Messiah who lays down his life in vicarious offering as a sacrifice for sin. In common with all humankind he dies a natural death.

In these writings, then, we have evidence of two originally distinct strands of eschatological expectation, sharing with each other certain common characteristics and becoming intertwined. Such an association, however, of Messiah and Son of Man would be confined to a relatively small group of apocalyptic writers, and in any case there would be no Son of Man doctrine in any way comparable with that of the traditional Messiah in Israel which would remain for the mass of the people the substance of their eschatological hope.

We have looked at the relationship between Messiah and Son of Man, but there is a third concept which must be taken into account and which is of considerable importance, not least for the Christian understanding of the messianic hope – the concept of the Suffering Servant of the Lord. Of particular interest in this regard is the language used of the Suffering Servant in Deutero-Isaiah and its echo in describing the Son of Man in Daniel and in the Similitudes of Enoch. In Daniel, for example, reference is made, as in Deutero-Isaiah, to 'the wise' and to 'the many' who suffer as the people of God at the hands of their foes; the Son of Man and the Suffering Servant, taken as collective figures, depict the same plight of the same people. So too with the Similitudes, language reminiscent of the Servant is used to describe the Son of Man: he is to be a 'staff for the righteous' and a 'light to the Gentiles', and each is chosen by God as the Lord's 'anointed'. But although the influence of the Servant passages is to be detected, the concept of atonement through vicarious suffering and death is altogether absent. In the Similitudes the Son of Man is presented as the judge of sinners; in Deutero-Isaiah the Servant suffers that others may live.

While suffering, though, may have been associated with the figure of the Messiah/Son of Man in the Jewish literature of this time, the notion of rejection by the people and forsakenness by God was quite unthinkable. That insight was to await one who was prepared to put such suffering to the test and thereby save his people from their sins.

(c) Jesus as Messiah/Son of Man

Jesus' followers hailed him as the promised Messiah and believed that in him the kingdom had come. It is not surprising, however, that Jesus himself was loath to use this title of himself, associated as it was with political overtones which contradicted his message and the task he had set himself to do. Indeed, it was not until near the close of his earthly life, when he stood confronted by the high priest, that he openly declared his messiahship (Mark 14.61f.). Even his own disciples would have failed to understand – as indeed Peter did at Caesarea Philippi. There he confessed Jesus as Messiah, but failed to appreciate that for him the Messiah must 'give his life a ransom for many' (Mark 10.45). By bringing together in this way the concepts of Davidic Messiah and of suffering as exemplified in the Servant Songs, Jesus gave an entirely new interpretation not only to ancient prophecy but also to the saviour of popular expectation. The way to deliverance was the way of rejection, suffering and death.

The familiar expression which Jesus used to express his divine calling was not Messiah but Son of Man. But here again he transformed its meaning and interpreted it messianically in terms of the Suffering Servant. The Son of Man 'must suffer many things . . . and be killed and on the third day rise again' (Mark 9.31).

All the indications are that in adopting the title 'Son of Man' Jesus was influenced by the occurrence of the expression in the Book of Daniel and by the promise there that 'dominion and glory and a kingdom' would be given to the Son of Man which would know no end. By adopting the title he expressed the belief that the promised kingdom was to find expression in his own life and ministry. Such a belief is certainly reflected in the conviction of the early church which firmly believed that the *eschaton* was bound up inseparably with their Master who, in his own person and work, was in a real sense the end of history. In him the messianic age had at last arrived.

This fact is demonstrated in at least three ways: first, in his power to forgive sins, one of the marks of the coming 'day of salvation' being that God would forgive the sins of his people; second, in his miracles of healing and exorcism which were demonstrations of the breaking in of 'the new age'; and third, in his death on the cross and his rising again from the dead. There is good cause to believe that Jesus saw fit to interpret the Son of Man as applied to himself in terms of the Suffering Servant and to see in his suffering and death the fulfilment of the kingdom. The Covenanters of Qumran had already seen their mission collectively in this light and sought through submission and suffering to make atonement for the sins of the people. Jesus now saw the mission of the Messiah/Son of Man/Suffering Servant fulfilled in himself.

Through him, and particularly through his death and resurrection, the powers of evil are routed. His crucifixion, we are told, is accompanied by strange, natural phenomena – an earthquake and the eclipse of the sun – for this Jesus is 'a man attested to you by God with mighty works and wonders and signs' (Acts 2.22). Following the 'messianic woes' of Gethsemane and Calvary the 'messianic secret' is revealed; with his resurrection and the coming of the Spirit it will at last become an 'open secret' and the kingdom will come 'with power' (Mark 9.1; cf. Romans 1.4). He will be exalted and be seen 'coming with the clouds of heaven' (Mark 14.62; cf. Daniel 7.13) and the kingdom will be consummated in his coming again to reign. In him the great day forecast by prophet and apocalyptist alike will at last have arrived. The kingdom has come; history has reached its goal and the whole creation waits with eager longing for 'the manifestation of the sons of God' (Romans 8.19).

2. THE LIFE TO COME

(a) The resurrection

The coming of the promised kingdom inevitably raised critical questions not only about its venue – on earth or in a supra-mundane world – but also about those who will take part in it. If it is for 'the righteous', what about those righteous men who have long-since died, some of them as martyrs for their religion? The old belief in Sheol is reflected in Ecclesiastes and in Ben Sira: the departed dwell as 'shades' – shadowy replicas of their former selves – in a land of oblivion and forgetfulness from which there is no return and this in turn is reflected in the belief of the Sadducees. In the Book of Wisdom, on the other hand, under the influence of Greek thought, the belief is expressed in the immortality of the soul after the death of the body: the righteous will be vindicated and the unrighteous punished.

Such a concept, however, was foreign to the Hebrew way of thinking altogether. For the Jew man is not a trichotomy of body, mind and spirit or a dichotomy of body and soul. He is a unity of personality in which 'body' plays a decisive part, animated by the breath-soul (Hebrew, *nephesh*) which comes from God. If he is really to survive as a true 'person', then that survival must be in the form of 'body', however that is to be defined. Within the Old Testament there are passages in Job (e.g. 14.13–15; 19.25–27) and the Psalms (e.g. 16, 49, 73), for example, where the writers' faith reaches out beyond the bounds of this life. But it is a faith that has not yet found an appropriate form in which to express itself. As H. Wheeler Robinson puts it, 'The religious experience of the Old Testament at its highest enters into a relation to God which is implicitly, if not explicitly, above that of time and space, though as yet unable to articulate itself without their aid.' Then he adds this: 'It is apocalyptic which provided the formula of resurrection for the nascent faith in something beyond death' (*Inspiration and Revelation in the Old Testament*, 1946, pp. 146f.).

At last a solution was found to the problem of the fate of the righteous and the wicked and an 'eschatology' of the individual was combined with that of the nation. The break-through came with the Book of Daniel or possibly with the somewhat earlier oracle embedded in the Book of Isaiah in chapters 24–27. The latter speaks of the dead arising. If this is a reference to individuals rather than to the nation as such, then it is the first allusion to bodily resurrection in the Old Testament and asserts that the pre-eminently righteous in Israel will be raised to share in the earthly messianic kingdom. More certain, however, is the reference in Daniel 12: 'And many of them that sleep in the dust of the earth shall awake, some to everlasting life and some to everlasting contempt' (12.2). Death would not rob the martyrs of their reward in the kingdom, nor would the tyrants escape the punishment that was their due. There are many variations in the apocalyptic writings that follow concerning those who are to be raised and in what form they will appear, but belief in the resurrection provided the key that helped to unlock a problem that had daunted generations past and opened the way for justice to be done to the wicked and the godly alike.

The Sadducees, as we have already noted, continued to follow the old belief in the survival of 'shades' in Sheol and rejected any belief in resurrection (cf. Acts 23.8; 26.8). The evidence of the Qumran Covenanters is rather ambiguous, but their belief no doubt corresponds to that of the Essenes as described by Josephus that bodies were perishable but souls sojourned in a realm of bliss or in a place of torment. The Pharisees, however, held fast to the resurrection belief and this became normative for Judaism in the generations that followed.

(b) 'Truncated' souls

The problems of participation in the kingdom and of rewards and punishment had found a solution in resurrection. But what of the state of the departed prior to that great day? This problem required yet another change in Hebrew thought. Hitherto personality was thought of as being wholly dependent on body, but now a continuity is recognized between life on this earth and life in Sheol. The dead as 'souls' survive as 'truncated' personalities, capable of knowledge and feeling, of pain and pleasure, but awaiting their fulfilment as persons in resurrection to receive the due rewards of their labours.

Thus, for many, Sheol becomes an intermediate abode where the souls of men await the resurrection. In certain books, as in Isaiah 24–27 and Daniel 12, the Old Testament-type Sheol is still recognizable. In others, speculation takes over and produces a whole variety of descriptions which defy definition. Writing of the *Christian* hope, Reinhold Niebuhr once warned, 'It is no part of Christian wisdom to presume a detailed knowledge of either the furniture of heaven or the temperature of hell.' This warning the apocalyptic writers failed to take! On the contrary, they extend the concept of Sheol in both directions, with Paradise at one end and

Hell at the other. The one may be a place of sensuous pleasure or spiritual communion; the other is a place of torment to which is given the name Gehenna, based on the *Ge Hinnom*, the rubbish dump south of Jerusalem where the city garbage was burned and the corpses of criminals left to rot.

In this concept of Sheol moral judgments and reactions are possible. What is more, in some of these writings at any rate, moral changes are also possible. Prayers for the dead are encouraged, for they may enable the righteous to enter into salvation (cf. Testament of Abraham 14). But in most of them no change is possible and no prayers will prevail: 'There shall not be there again . . . change of ways, nor place for prayer, nor sending of petitions, nor receiving of knowledge, nor giving of love, nor place for repentance' (II Baruch 85.12).

(c) The resurrection body

The nature of the resurrection body itself is also a subject of much speculation in these writings. For the most part it would seem that it is of such a kind that it corresponds to the nature of the kingdom in which the resurrected righteous are privileged to share. Thus, in the Book of Daniel where the kingdom is both earthly and eternal, the body in question is physical and material and its duration eternal. This is the picture conveyed by other later apocalyptic writings and also by such a passage as II Maccabees 7.10f., where it is reported of one of the seven martyred brothers in the time of the Maccabees, 'when it was demanded, he quickly put out his tongue and courageously stretched forth his hands, and said nobly, I got these from heaven . . . and from him I hope to get them back again' (cf. also 14.46).

The writer of II Baruch, among others, is puzzled by these things. He asks their meaning and how those who are resurrected will 'resume this form of the present and put on these entramelling members' (49.3). We are reminded vividly of Paul's words in I Corinthians 15.35ff., which reflect the same kinds of questions in the Christian church and the same kinds of answers given in II Baruch. Elsewhere the resurrection body is a 'spiritual' body, corresponding to its 'spiritual' environment either in a transformed earth or in the age to come. These 'spiritual bodies' are variously described as 'garments of glory' or 'garments of light' or being 'like the angels in heaven' or 'shining like the stars'. They are represented as 'transformed' physical bodies – 'sown a natural body, raised a spiritual body' (cf. I Cor. 15.42ff.) or counterparts in Paradise of the earthly body or as developing alongside and with the other.

(d) The final judgment

Mention is frequently made of the final judgment to which the whole universe is moving and in which righteousness will at last find its vindication. Sometimes this takes the form of a judgment on the nations either at a crisis point in history or in the shape of a Great Assize when they wil be judged by God or by his Messiah. More often than not it precedes the messianic kingdom; in other cases it follows this and precedes the age to come. Sometimes the judgment falls on the Gentiles; at other times on Jews and Gentiles alike. Sometimes it is confined to nations and wicked men; at other times angels and demons come under the divine wrath. Sometimes Israel is judged with no quarter given; at other times there is opportunity for repentance. Sometimes the Gentiles are utterly condemned; at others a place is offered them in the coming kingdom.

But, as we have seen, in these writings there is an increasing emphasis on the individual and his share in the kingdom through resurrection. So also is there a process of individualization in the case of final judgment. As in Sheol following the time of death so now, moral judgments matter and men are to be judged for the deeds done in the flesh. Sometimes the judgment begins in Gehenna itself: 'Recline in anguish and rest in torment till thy last time come, in which thou wilt come again, and be tormented still more' (II Baruch 36.11). At other times it comes at the final judgment: 'Every weight, every measure, and every makeweight will be as in the market . . . and everyone shall learn his own measure, and according to his measure shall take his reward' (II Enoch 44.5). Each one will answer on the day of judgment for his own sin, 'for then everyone shall bear his own righteousness or unrighteousness' (II Esdras 7.102ff.).

Out of this medley of speculation concerning 'the last things' comes the assurance that God is just, that life and death are in his hands and that he is sovereign Lord not only of men and nations but of all created things.

(e) The Christian hope

Early Judaism and the early church in many respects shared a common background of belief in the resurrection and the future hope. The big difference between them was the claim, on which the entire Christian faith stood, that Jesus the Messiah had in fact risen from the dead and was seated at the right hand of God the Father. Indeed Paul, writing to the church in Corinth, goes so far as to say, 'If Christ has not been raised, then . . . your faith is in vain' (1 Corinthians 15.14). In him, as we have seen, the kingdom had begun to break in; in his resurrection it was seen to come 'with power' (Mark 9.1; cf. Romans 1.4); and in his *parousia* it will be consummated in his coming again to reign.

Another difference is that in the Christian hope those who believe in Christ share now in his resurrection, have entered now into the kingdom, experience now the blessings of the age to come. 'Eternal life' is a quality of life which is a reality here as well as hereafter. To be 'in Christ' at this moment and to be 'with Christ' at the end are of one piece. To be 'absent from the body' is to be 'present with the Lord' (II Corinthians 5.8). Having been buried with him in baptism, the believer is already raised with him into newness of life (cf. Romans 6.4) and has entered into the blessings of the age to come. This will reach its cosummation at the *parousia*, which will mark the end of history and the full flowering of the age to come (cf. I Corinthians 15.51ff.).

As we have seen, Paul and his fellow Christians wrestled with the same questions that confronted his Jewish contemporaries concerning the nature of the resurrection body and shared in large measure the convictions they expressed (cf. I Corinthians 15.35ff.). He concludes with them that 'death is swallowed up in victory'. The source of that victory he longs they might make their own: 'Thanks be to God who gives us the victory through our Lord Jesus Christ' (1 Corinthians 15.54ff.).

For Further Reading

Texts

Charles, R. H. (ed.), *The Apocrypha and Pseudepigrapha of the Old Testament*, 2 vols, OUP 1913

Charlesworth, J. H. (ed.), *The Old Testament Pseudepigrapha*, 2 vols, Darton, Longman and Todd and Doubleday 1983 and 1986

Nickelsburg, G. W. E., *Jewish Literature between the Bible and the Mishnah*, SCM Press and Fortress Press 1981

Sparkes, H. F. D. (ed.), *The Apocryphal Old Testament*, Clarendon Press 1984

Vermes, G., *The Dead Sea Scrolls in English*, Penguin 1982

Colson, F. H., and Whitaker, G. H. (eds), *Philo*, Heinemann (Loeb Classical Library), 1929–1943

Thackery, H.St. J., Marcus, R., and Feldman, L. (eds), *Josephus*, Heinemann (Loeb Classical Library) 1926–65

Danby, H., *The Mishnah*, Clarendon Press 1933

General Background and Introduction

Bruce, F. F., *New Testament History*, Nelson 1969

Foerster, W., *Palestinian Judaism in New Testament Times*, Oliver and Boyd 1964

Grant, F. C., *Roman Hellenism and the New Testament*, Oliver and Boyd 1962

Hengel, Martin, *Judaism and Hellenism*, SCM Press and Fortress Press 1974

Leaney, A. R. C., *The Jewish and Christian World*, 200 BC to AD 200, CUP 1984

FOR FURTHER READING

Metzger, Bruce M., *An Introduction to the Apocrypha*, OUP 1957
Moore, G. F., *Judaism in the First Centuries of the Christian Era*, 3 vols, Harvard University Press, Cambridge, Mass. 1927–30
Pfeiffer, R. H., *History of New Testament Times*, with an Introduction to the Apocrypha, Harper 1949
Russell, D. S., *Between the Testaments*, SCM Press and Fortress Press 1960
Russell, D. S., *The Jews from Alexander to Herod*, OUP 1967
Schürer, E. (revd by Vermes, G. and Miller, F.), *The History of the Jewish People in the Age of Jesus Christ*, 3 vols, T & T Clark 1971 onwards

Apocalyptic

Hanson, P. D., *The Dawn of Apocalyptic*, Fortress Press 1975
Koch, K., *The Rediscovery of Apocalyptic*, SCM Press 1972
Rowland, C., *The Open Heaven*, SPCK 1982
Rowley, H. H., *The Relevance of Apocalyptic*, revd edn Lutterworth 1963
Russell, D. S., *The Method and Message of Jewish Apocalyptic*, SCM Press and Westminster Press, Philadelphia, 1964

Judaism and Christianity

Davies, W. D., *Paul and Rabbinic Judaism*, SPCK 1958
Davies, W. D., *Christian Origins and Judaism*, Darton, Longman and Todd 1962
Grant, F. C., *Ancient Judaism and the New Testament*, Oliver and Boyd 1960
Johnson, S. E., *Jesus in his Homeland*, Scribner, N Y 1957
Parkes, J., *The Foundations of Judaism and Christianity*, Valentine Mitchell 1960
Riches, J., *Jesus and the Transformation of Judaism*, Darton, Longman and Todd 1980
Sander, E. P., *Paul and Palestinian Judaism*, SCM Press and Fortress Press 1977

Sanders, E. P., *Paul, the Law and the Jewish People*, Fortress Press 1983 and SCM Press 1985

Sanders, E. P., *Jesus and Judaism*, SCM Press and Fortress Press 1985

Vermes, G., *Jesus the Jew*, 2nd edn SCM Press and Fortress Press 1983

Vermes, G., *Jesus and the World of Judaism*, SCM Press and Fortress Press 1983

Index of Texts

I The Old Testament

II Apocrypha and Pseudepigrapha of the Old Testament

INDEX OF TEXTS

141

Index of Subjects

144

INDEX OF SUBJECTS

Index of Modern Scholars